AMERICA'S
FIRST WOMAN
WARRIOR

A AMERICA'S
FIRST WOMAN
WARRIOR

THE
COURAGE
OF
DEBORAH SAMPSON

LUCY FREEMAN
AND
ALMA HALBERT BOND, Ph.D.

PARAGON
HOUSE
NEW YORK

First edition, 1992

Published in the United States by
Paragon House
90 Fifth Avenue
New York, N.Y. 10011

Manufactured in the United States of America

Library of Congress Cataloging-in-Publication Data

Freeman, Lucy.
    America's first woman warrior : the courage of Deborah Sampson /
Lucy Freeman and Alma Halbert Bond. — 1st ed.
        p.   cm.
    Includes bibliographical references and index.
    ISBN 1 – 55778 – 514 – 7 : $22.95
    1. Gannett, Deborah Sampson, 1760–1827.   2. Soldiers—United
States—Biography.   3. Women soldiers—United States—Biography.
4. United States—History—Revolution, 1775–1783—Participation,
Female.   I. Title.
E276.G36F74   1992
973.3'092—dc20
[B]   91–24596
                                                         CIP

This book is dedicated to Dale Schroedel, my niece, who, twelve years ago, after we flew to Boston, drove our rental car to Plymouth, Plympton, and Sharon, all in east Massachusetts, as we searched for knowledge about the life of America's first heroine. On a second trip, Dale, today a lawyer and a private investigator, drove us from New York to West Point, where we obtained a description of the place as it was in 1782 and saw where our remarkable woman served a year and a half in the army. Dale not only helped make the two journeys enjoyable but appeared to get as much pleasure as I did in uncovering the exciting life of the amazing Deborah Sampson.

CONTENTS

ACKNOWLEDGMENTS

The authors wish to thank, first and foremost, PJ Dempsey, senior editor at Paragon House, for encouraging them to write this book and for helping in its formation. They also thank Edward Paige, managing editor, and Christopher O'Connell, assistant editor, for their welcome contributions. Thanks also go to Jane Dystel, our literary agent, for her belief in the book.

Among those who helped us uncover the facts of Deborah Sampson's life are Charles Bricknell, historian, of Plympton, Massachusetts; Mrs. Robert Cartwright, secretary of the Sharon Historical Commission and Florence Gannett Moody and Eleanor Moody Connors, of Sharon, great-great-granddaughters of Deborah Sampson.

For the description of West Point in 1782 and 1783, we are indebted to Alan C. Aimone, Military History librarian at the United States Military Academy and Robert E. Schnare, assistant librarian for Special Collections at the United States Military Academy.

We also thank Mrs. Florence S. Mendall, chief librarian of the Plympton Public Library; Elizabeth Farrar, director, Mrs. Helen

Goodyear, reference librarian in charge of historical collections and Clara Hayes, all of the Sharon Public Library; Mrs. Eleanor Thompkins, librarian of the Middleborough Public Library; Muriel N. Peters, librarian of the Dedham Historical Society; Gordon Marshall, assistant librarian of the Library Company of Philadelphia; Joseph J. Felcone, librarian of the David Library of the American Revolution, Washington Crossing, Pennsylvania; the Library of the Historical Society of New York and the Library of the Historical Society of Pennsylvania.

PROLOGUE

In the history of our country only one woman, disguised as a man, officially served as a soldier in the Continental Army during the Revolutionary War. She was acknowledged as a warrior by the United States government and, through an act of Congress, became the first woman to be placed on the pension list.

Her name was Deborah Sampson.

Who was Deborah Sampson? And why was she, among all the women of America, the only one to join the armed forces in the guise of a man, becoming the country's first feminist?

Why has a definitive biography of Deborah Sampson never been published, particularly in this day of feminist heroines? There was the biography written in 1797 by Herman Mann, a printer and writer, titled *The Female Review or Memoirs of an American Young Lady*. There have appeared two fictional books for the young adult: Cora Cheney wrote *The Incredible Deborah* (Scribner's, 1967) and Florence Parker Simister wrote *Girl With a Musket* (Hastings House, 1959).

There are, however, enough facts to draw valid conclusions about Deborah's life. It is clear she was America's first feminist, even though she joined the ranks of the army surreptitiously in the garb of a man, asking for equality with men.

In her way she differed from other prominent feminists. Joan of Arc heard voices and was in all likelihood psychotic. Virginia Woolf, who committed suicide when she could not cope with reality, had an illustrious father who served as mentor and guide, whereas Deborah lost her father when she was four-and-a-half years old. Women today have the feminist movement to promote their search for equality. But it took someone with a core of steel to defy the dictates of society in 1782 and tread a dangerous trail that could have destroyed her. Deborah Sampson created history when she left family and home without anyone's support to embark on her voyage to a lasting fame.

Where did she get such strength? What can we learn from her story to help other women attain their potential? The answers appear in the following history of her life.

This book includes Dr. Alma Halbert Bond's moving and expert interpretation of Deborah Sampson's recurrent nightmare that she reported to her first biographer, Herman Mann. Dr. Bond, a prominent psychoanalyst, reveals how this nightmare, along with Deborah's childhood memories, which she also told Mann, unearthed the most powerful wishes and fears of her life. It also explains why she wished to serve in the Revolutionary War.

This is an important approach to biography, as our dreams and memories do not lie—the psychological truth is imbedded in them for all who have eyes to see. Freud revealed the theory that through dreams we unearth our buried secrets. Just as the tides of the sea hurl upon the sands the material which the mighty ocean hoards, the unconscious part of our mind thrusts forth in a dream what the conscious denies. Recurrent dreams, as Deborah's were, tell of the dreamer's most vital conflicts.

The true story of Deborah's life includes many of her early

memories as told to Mann, as well as important material supplied by Charles H. Bricknell, noted historian, and research by the authors of this book. Lucy Freeman visited the house where Deborah was born, which still stands in Plympton, Massachusetts, not far from Plymouth. She also visited Rock Ridge Cemetery, in Sharon, Massachusetts, where Deborah was buried under the shade of the "third maple down," between the graves of her husband and son.

Many women today fight for the right to bear arms as they join the United States Army. This story of the courage and valor of Deborah Sampson fits in with their search for equality.

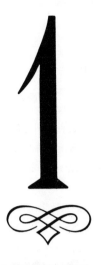

THE DISAPPEARANCE OF DEBORAH SAMPSON

Early in May, 1782—the exact date remains unknown—a twenty-two-year-old woman named Deborah Sampson living in Middleborough, Massachusetts, fourteen miles from Plymouth, where America's first settlers landed, took off her feminine attire and stepped into a man's suit.

There exist two versions as to how she procured such an outfit. The first holds that she spun and wove the cloth, then took it to the local tailor to make a suit for a gentleman her size. She pretended it was a gift for a relative leaving home to join the Continental Army. General George Washington had just issued a plea for twenty thousand more volunteers to join the fight against the British.

The second version maintains that she not only spun the threads and wove the material but cut and sewed the suit, keeping it hidden from all eyes. She had a reputation as the most skilled hand at the loom in the area. This talent extended to sewing as well.

Deborah was boarding at the home of Captain and Mrs. Benjamin Leonard, whose son Samuel had enlisted in the army the year before. She had supported herself for the past three years by teaching school in the summer and spinning wool at the homes of Middleborough families in the winter. She lived with them until their clothing requirements were met, then moved to the next house that needed her services.

The evening she changed her attire from a woman's to a man's, she first enjoyed a dinner of baked ham, turnips, potatoes and apple pie, cooked by Mrs. Leonard. Deborah ate everything on her plate, knowing she would need the sustenance.

Once upstairs in her small bedroom, she closed the door. She crossed to the looking glass on top of the chest that contained her clothes. She stared solemnly for one last glimpse at an image of herself soon to disappear.

She saw blue eyes, blond hair soft and fine, drawn straight behind her ears, hanging in thick curls to her waist. She was not beautiful but her features were appealing and regular, as shown in a portrait later painted when she was forty.

Her mouth was of average size, her nose had a noble, slightly Romanesque cast. Her skin was white and soft in spite of years of bathing with lye soap. When younger, she had tanned every summer from outdoor work. People told her she had a low, appealing voice, unlike the submissive whine of some women of that era obeying commands of husbands they feared. Deborah was described as serious and thoughtful but possessing at times a dreamy air, lost in the clouds of memory.

She was tall for a woman of those days, five feet, nine inches, as compared to the average woman's height of four feet, seven inches. Her figure was sturdy, stolid. She carried herself erect, whether moving across a parlor or a field. Years of driving cows to pasture, churning butter, chopping wood, pitching hay, riding the horses to town or behind the plough, feeding chickens and pigs, had given her firm hips, strong arms and legs. The long blond curls, soft white skin and low appealing voice made it difficult to think of her as possessing a masculine demeanor.

The man's suit lay on her bed. It was made of brown fustian, a coarse cotton twill fabric. Beside it spread a man's ruffled white shirt, white handkerchief, brown hat and whaleskin wallet, all bought at various stores in town. Her farm boots sat on the floor by the bed.

With what must have been excitement mixed with trepidation, she stepped toward the bed. She removed her undergarments and her shoes. She kept on her white socks—men and women both wore socks at that time.

Her naked breasts were not large, but she had to find some way to conceal their normal feminine fullness. She walked to the chest, opened it and took out a piece of white linen cloth three feet long and six inches wide. She wrapped it tightly around her breasts like a bandage, knotting it at the back.

Steeling herself, Deborah seized a pair of scissors and cut her curly blond locks to shoulder-length, like a man's. She then smoothed her hair to the masculine "flat top." Men at that time wore their hair long on the sides and, fortunately for Deborah, without sideburns.

For her final change, she slipped her arms into the man's ruffled shirt, then donned breeches, waistcoat, outer coat and hat before she stepped into her farm boots. Except for the boots, the outfit was partly that of a dapper gentleman of fashion, partly of a young man of business.

As she stared at herself in the large looking glass, Deborah felt conflicting emotions. On one hand, a moment of sadness in surrendering her lovely curls and feminine identity. On the other, a laugh of delight and defiance at the idea of pulling off her disguise. She made quite a handsome man, her legs long and slim in the breeches.

She wondered what her mother, a practical but often frightened woman, would think. She would believe her daughter had gone stark mad at the age of twenty-two not to marry the young man living four miles away in Plympton who had fallen in love with her.

But Deborah felt no sign of love for him. She did not wish to be part of a love that seemed like a short fit of epilepsy, a love used only to ease the hunger of lust. She yearned for a love that held respect and friendship as well as sensual need. She did not believe she had to get married by hook or crook, like many of her contemporaries. She considered such an act embarrassing, like selling herself to the highest bidder.

Some of her friends had fallen desperately in love with a gilt coat, a scarlet hat or a false, soft word. Deborah yearned for a man with substance, a man who might set up a hospital, for instance, or endow a school—the type of man she had not yet met. She believed her friends who had married out of sudden passion or because they wanted a husband to support them fell into a slumber that would be permanent. She thought a woman died in mind and body if she looked no higher in her aspirations than her fantasy, not seeing the man as he was.

On this momentous night in May, excited at her daring plans, Deborah temporarily put aside her feeling of sadness at the open loss of her femininity. She walked around the room convincing herself the garments of a man were much more comfortable to wear and easier to move in. She placed twelve dollars—all the money she possessed—in a pocket of her waistcoat. Then she sat by the window, listening for the closing of the bedroom door down the hall.

She thought Mr. and Mrs. Leonard would be asleep by ten. When her silver watch showed that hour, she stealthily opened the door as though planning to rob the poor box at the First Congregational Church.

She crept quietly across the wide wooden planks of the hall, then tiptoed down the stairs. She opened the front door (never locked), wincing as it creaked. She wondered if her career as soldier would be stopped before it even started. But when no one appeared she stepped out the door, closing it carefully behind her for what proved forever.

She had lived in the town of Middleborough ever since she was ten years old. Since her mother had, as Deborah thought of it, given her away to a farmer, his wife and ten sons.

But now, after all the uncertain years, she was on her way to a new life. A life she planned to live as a man fighting the enemy trying to destroy America.

ROBERT SHURTLIFF IS REBORN

In the dark of night Deborah headed for Taunton, ten miles to the west of Middleborough. The farm boots were heavy on her feet, not fashioned for long journeys over rutted dirt roads once trod by Indian moccasins, then the heavy shoes of white settlers, the hooves of horses and finally the wheels of farm carts and stagecoaches.

The warm suit lovingly woven by her eager fingers kept out the chill of that May night. Thick clouds hid the moon but she preferred the dark where no one was likely to recognize her.

It would be a lonely walk but she had taken many a lonely walk, often her only moments of privacy. She had always felt at home in the midst of the tall pines, the spruce, the maple, the walnut and the black, red and white oaks whose needles and leaves gave the countryside its different tones of green. If she had been born a man, she thought, she would have set out to the frontier, carving the country's way to the West.

With her farmer's strength and vibrant youth, she walked all night. She saw ahead the green fields of Taunton as the first rays of the sun lit the dark sky. She thought of the many mornings she was up with the lark's song, heard the rooster's crow as she scattered corn to the chickens or led the cows to pasture in her second home with the farmer, his wife and ten sons.

In Taunton, all was silent. Then suddenly she heard footsteps. A stocky man walked toward her as she felt her first moment of panic. Would it be someone who knew her? The figure neared and she recognized a neighboring farmer, William Bennett, who sometimes nodded to her as they passed on the road. If he saw through her disguise, she was lost.

This test was the important one. She was forced to meet the enemy head on. Heart racing, she looked squarely into his eyes and waited. He stared at her as though she were a stranger. She sighed in relief, realizing he probably never would associate her with an early morning, itinerant stroller in Taunton, where he delivered milk and eggs daily.

She had come through her first crisis without being revealed. Feeling this deserved a celebration, she walked to a tavern that kept open through the night for travelers midway between Plymouth and Providence. Then came a shock. The man who took her order for bacon, eggs, biscuits and tea treated her like another man, called her "sir." She realized that people who looked at her now saw not Deborah Sampson but a strange young man. She would have to get rid of her lifelong awareness of herself as a woman.

With her twelve dollars diminished by the cost of the tasty breakfast, she frugally stuffed the remaining biscuits in her pocket as rations for the rest of the day.

Suddenly she felt Mr. Bennett might have had second thoughts about her, become suspicious and called for someone to pursue her. She decided to change the direction of her flight. She followed the stagecoach road southeast to New Bedford, twenty-five miles away. It was a seaport town she had always wanted to explore. Two years before it had been beseiged by the British.

She walked until dark took over. Feeling fatigued, without sleep for twenty-four hours, she turned toward an obscure path off the main highway that led into a thicket. The boughs of a large elm served as canopy as she fell asleep, head propped against the trunk. She was too exhausted to give a thought to the soft bed she had left behind.

The next morning she reached New Bedford. The once-flourishing seaport was pulling itself together after the British had sent barges up the estuary, laid to ashes all the ships in the harbor and nearly extinguished the village. The residents now did not possess a single piece of artillery or bayonet to oppose the invaders.

Deborah walked down the hill to the harbor, listened to the raucous cry of gulls, breathed deeply of the salt air tangy with the odor of freshly caught fish. She wandered along the wharves filled with schooners that would soon sail in search of cod, salmon, mackerel and whales. The whales provided oil for candles and lamps that transformed the cottages of New England farmers from dark cells into lighted rooms where young girls like herself stayed up nights to read of other lives, other worlds.

She stared in wonder at the shipyards down which slipped sloops and schooners large enough to sail the seven seas. The forests of New England furnished oak for the timbers and boards, firs for the masts, pitch for the turpentine and tar. The fields yielded hemp for the ropes, the mines gave up iron for the anchors and chains. The nearby ocean offered itself to young men eager to escape the fate of the farmer struggling to make a living off the stony fields.

Deborah thought of her father, one of the adventurers who turned their backs on farming, sought their fortunes on the sea. She remembered her father's cousin, Captain Simeon Sampson, of Kingston, Massachusetts, who had escaped by dressing as a woman after being held hostage on a Plymouth merchantman captured by the French during the French and Indian wars. When he received the first Continental Navy Commission in 1775 and was placed in charge of what then passed for a navy in America, he became a hero in the eyes of her family as well as the world. Remembering how he had escaped the enemy by dressing as a *woman* she now wondered if she had thought of dressing like a man in order to *fight* the enemy. Nothing else in her life had applied to cross-dressing.

Captain Sampson had been in command of the brigantine *Independence*, the first privateer fitted out by Massachusetts. Once when he visited her father, Deborah, at the age of four-and-a-half, remembered innocently asking if she could be his cabin boy.

Despite his own successful attempt at cross-dressing, the captain was not sympathetic. He roared with laughter, said she was too young to be a cabin boy. Then he told her in a serious tone no matter how old she became he would not be allowed to accept her as a member of the navy because she was a girl. This must have proved somewhat of a challenge to her—if he could cross-dress, why couldn't she?

Of the myriad of fleeting moments Deborah could have remembered from her early life, why did this incident remain so strongly?

Each memory we retain from childhood is fraught with meaning, preserved for life because it contains powerful emotions vital in the development of our personality.

Deborah no doubt chose to remember the incident at this time because it had occurred at a fateful moment that determined much of her future, including her subsequent army career. Any drastic step we take, whether murder or marching to war in the uniform of the opposite sex, stems from childhood desires that were frustrated.

Deborah had felt deep grief at being publicly derogated by her uncle. She recalled standing red-faced, shriveled in humiliation. She became aware for the first time that being a girl would keep her from doing many important things her four brothers were permitted to do. Equally embarrassing was the fact that her uncle's ridicule had exposed her "deficiency" for the world to see.

Deborah's later history suggests that deep within, this gallant little girl vowed that when she grew up she would not allow her femininity to deter her from the world she wished to enter. That somehow, someday, she would find a way to avenge her humiliation and join the exalted world of men.

Nothing less than a career in the Continental Army would serve to undo the catastrophic emotional damage caused by her uncle's early belittling remarks. When Deborah was accepted for service by the Continental Army, she was getting even for the mortifying scene of her uncle's rejection. She was accepted as a man, capable of fighting for her country. She must have felt tremendous triumph at this long-delayed acceptance. Now she would not be considered inferior to a man.

Starved after eating only biscuits for the past twenty-four hours, Deborah again sought food in a tavern. While waiting for her order of fried clams, she daringly asked for a flip, made of rum, molasses and beer. The sugar and molasses came from the West Indies and New England distilleries transformed the products into a drink that was pure liquid fire. Both men and women drank wine, beer and rum, shunning the waters of America as a carrier of disease. Every general store sold casks of rum, gin and tubs of punch.

As she sipped away at the flip, a bronzed, bearded sailor sauntered over. He asked if she would go to sea as a waiter on his ship, sailing the next day for the West Indies. He added the captain would even advance part of the wages, as he was eager to obtain such a handsome, strong young man for his vessel.

For a moment Deborah felt tempted, exhilarated by the success of her disguise, as well as the rum. It would be exciting to spend a month sailing to London as her father had once done regularly. But a wiser inner voice urged her to think it over and she told the sailor she needed time to decide. He said he would return within half an hour for her answer.

Another man who had heard the conversation walked over and warned her the captain of this ship had the reputation of being brutal, beating his crew and starving them. Deborah gratefully thanked the stranger and gulped down her clams, wanting to be gone before the bearded sailor returned.

She ran from the tavern, up the hill and out of New Bedford. She felt another thrill of triumph in that the sailor had believed her a fit and healthy young man, willing to trust her to do a man's work aboard ship. The humiliating effects of her Uncle Simeon's insults were overcome at last. She glowed with new confidence in her ability to handle a man's garb. She was amazed at how quickly men accepted her as one of them.

But perhaps it was not so amazing since, from the age of ten to eighteen, she had lived in a farmhouse with ten boys who chivalrously accepted her as one of them. And before that she had four brothers—a fifth had died just before she was born—to teach her their masculine ways.

Now she completely reversed her route. Undaunted by the distance, she headed north toward Boston, seventy miles away, intending when she arrived there to find a recruiting army station where she could offer her services.

One evening she slept on a bank of moss in the woods, framed by wild orchids of pale green and white and purple violets. During the day she passed field after field separated by fences or stone walls, though there were miles she saw not a farmhouse, not a face. She watched the shadows of the hills at dusk darken the greens and yellows of pastures and meadows. One night, weary of the hardships of the road and the woods, she treated herself to a soft bed at a tavern, where she ate supper and used the facilities to wash her hands and face.

Finally, from a distance, she saw for the first time the church spires of the city that sparked America's fight for freedom. She often wanted to visit Boston but lacked the money. She had read in the *Boston Gazette*, one of her major sources of news, that the city with its 15,500 inhabitants was now the third largest in the colonies. Philadelphia with 40,000 was first and New York with 22,000, second.

Massachusetts with 355,000 residents, boasted the largest white population of all the colonies although if slaves were included, Virginia with its 500,000 occupants ranked higher. There were 3,000,000 people in America at this time, including 600,000 slaves and 1,000,000 Indians. Of the settlers, about sixty percent were English. Of these, fourteen percent were Scotch-Irish. The next largest group, the Germans, constituted eight percent of the population. Deborah knew the statistics well for she had taught them to her classes during the summer school sessions even though they were not part of prescribed lessons.

Deborah first entered Boston on the Middle Post Road, according to Herman Mann's version of her recollections. She walked the cobbled streets, saw Faneuil Hall, King's Chapel and the Customs House. She peered reverently into the window of Paul Revere's silver shop. (She would later meet him and he would come to her rescue in a gallant way.) She walked to the Beacon Street home of her other hero, John Hancock. She had admired him ever since he, the wealthiest man in the state, had said at the time the British attacked Boston, "Burn Boston and make John Hancock a beggar if the public good requires it." She also admired him for being the first to sign the Declaration of Independence, writing in letters so large that he said King George could read his name without glasses.

She came upon Christ Church, recalling the one lit lantern in its steeple that warned the British were coming by land on the night of April 19, 1775, carrying Major Pitcairn's demand at Lexington that "the damned rebels disperse." When they refused to do so, the redcoats fired "the shot heard 'round the world," leaving eight men dead.

Deborah gazed at elegant houses in which, she knew, lived young women of wealth and charm with all the social graces and a delicate, self-effacing manner toward men. She felt a twinge of regret at the choice that pressed her onward toward hardship and danger. She imagined what the young wealthy women would think of her—she who had grown up spreading fertilizer on fields of flax and scything hay and was now giving up the pleasures of youth and femininity, perhaps forever if a British bullet killed her as she set forth on a dangerous mission.

She passed the shops of tailors, weavers, shoemakers, bakers, once the poor and oppressed of Europe, now treated as equals entitled to property and the protection of the law. Many had spent a few years as indentured servants, as she had, to pay for their passage. And now their new freedom was threatened by a tyrant three thousand miles away.

After a few days of further exploration, eating very sparsely for her funds were slowly disappearing, Deborah left Boston. She walked southwest through Roxbury, Dedham and Madfield before she enlisted in the army, wanting to see more of the state where her heroic ancestors had battled to survive their enemies—the icy winter weather and the hostile Indians. *Her* enemies consisted of fifty thousand redcoats, twenty-nine thousand paid mercenary Hessians and eight thousand five hundred loyalist volunteers called Tories.

She reached Bellingham on the border, just north of Rhode Island, 40 miles directly west of Middleborough, but 150 miles as she had walked it, evidence of her farm girl strength and inborn vigor. She passed the Baptist Church where the Reverend Noah Alden preached regularly. He had helped convert her to a Baptist when he visited his birthplace in Middleborough. They were both descendants of Priscilla and John Alden, which now made her feel she had a relative in town. But she dared not risk visiting him for he would recognize her, though she yearned for the momentary comfort of sitting in a home, perhaps even to ask for a loan. She was down to her last few pennies.

Tired and hungry, she spent them all for corncakes, molasses and a cup of tea in a tavern. As she sat savoring the tea, a strange man approached her.

He asked if she had ever been in the army. At first she felt startled, as at New Bedford. But then she felt a moment of triumph, realizing her disguise was still successful. She told him she was not a veteran.

He then urged her to enlist, explaining she would see the rest of the states at no cost and receive food, lodging and uniform free—plus a large bounty of sixty pounds, almost two hundred dollars in continental currency. A small share of the bounty would go to him, he added, since he was a speculator and entitled to this pittance by enlisting her. She would be part of the quota for Uxbridge, a nearby town. He offered to drive her to Worcester, twenty miles to the west, where she could enlist.

Deborah did not mind giving him part of the bounty. He would make it easier for her to achieve her long desired mission. There was nothing to spend money for anyway once she was in the army.

She knew cash bounties were offered by the localities to persuade men to enlist or reenlist. Many had served two- and three-year terms, then returned home. The male population of every town capable of bearing arms was divided into classes according to property and wealth. Each class was obliged to furnish a soldier for the army. A man's class determined the amount of his bounty. Substitutes from other areas could be hired to fill the quota. Many men signed up, accepted the cash bounty, then deserted to register in another area to acquire a second bounty. For this reason the Tories called the Continental Army "a contemptible body of vagrants, deserters and thieves." But these vagrants, deserters and thieves seemed to be winning the war.

Still a bit apprehensive about her chances of entering the army, Deborah asked if she would have to pass any physical examination. The speculator said the muster captain just looked a man over carefully, known as "passing muster," then decided whether he was fit. He added the army was so desperate for men they were practically taking skeletons.

Congress did not possess the power to draft an army. It could only ask for volunteers to serve for a certain length of time. The year before it had requested thirty-seven thousand men but only eight thousand responded. Enlistments had dropped sharply because soldiers were not paid, food was meager and epidemics of smallpox, malignant fever and other diseases swept through the camps regularly. New England had always contributed far more than its share of fighting men and recruiters in Massachusetts were working overtime to raise the number needed.

The speculator led Deborah to a horse and cart, then set out for Worcester. On arrival they stopped in front of a small house that served as office for the army. They walked into a room and the speculator introduced Deborah to a man in an officer's uniform seated behind a desk. His name was Captain Eliphalet Thorp, chairman of Class Number Two for Uxbridge.

Captain Thorp first asked Deborah her age. She paused, then said in as masculine a tone as she could muster, keeping her voice low, that she was seventeen. She had to lie because she could never produce a beard, not even a stubble of one.

Then the captain asked gruffly, "Have you ever fired a musket?"

"I've hunted deer, wild turkey and rabbit," she replied. She was proud of her ability to take aim and shoot accurately.

The interview seemed to be going well. But she waited with trepidation for his decision. Was Captain Thorp another Captain Simeon Sampson? Was this to be a dreaded repetition of her first rejection from the armed forces of the United States when she was informed at the age of four-and-a-half that no women were accepted?

Captain Thorp lifted an official looking document from a pile of papers on his desk. It was headed *Articles of Enlistment*. He slowly wrote in the date, May 20, 1782. Indicating a blank space, he asked her to sign. The enlistment was for three years.

Deborah sighed in relief, took up the pen. She felt the many years of humiliation as a subservient female were avenged at last.

Her enlistment paper exists today, on file in the office of the Secretary of the Commonwealth of Massachusetts. It shows she gave herself the first and middle name of her oldest brother, who had died at the age of eight, just before her birth.

She was now Robert Shurtliff.

3

NO TIME FOR FEAR

Deborah marched out of Worcester in a regiment worthy of her valor. She was one of fifty new recruits of the fourth Massachusetts Regiment of the Continental Army.

This historic regiment was formed in April 1775, from twelve militia minutemen companies of Worcester County who had responded to the Lexington Alarm under Colonel Ebenezer Learned. Learned had to resign as commander in May 1776 because of ill health. Lieutenant Colonel William Shepard, who fought and was wounded in the Battle of Long Island, was now in command.

The recruits would be led by Sergeant William Gambel, dispatched from the army training post at West Point. Their two-hundred mile march over the Berkshire Hills of western Massachusetts would take them south through Connecticut to New York State and their destination: the military fortress at West Point. This would be Deborah's home for the next year-and-a-half.

She had no idea what had been happening in the war and was grateful when Sergeant Gambel informed the recruits of the latest news as they stopped to rest by the wayside or eat at a tavern.

Fourteen miles north of West Point, in Newburgh, General Washington had established his headquarters and residence on March 31, 1782 after passing the winter in Philadelphia. He had stationed the main force of the Continental Army, about nine thousand men, in the neighboring town of New Windsor, also on the Hudson River. A few token troops were scattered in camps from Fort Edward, New York, to Charleston, South Carolina.

After the battle of Yorktown, when British General Charles Cornwallis was defeated on October 19, 1781, the French troops, which had taken part with spectacular success in their only combat of the war, joining late, remained in the south but were expected to encamp near West Point in late spring.

Standing proud and tall in her finely cut, tailored fustian suit, Deborah was the best-dressed of the newly enlisted soldiers marching four abreast down the highway. Most of them looked as if they too had grown up on Massachusetts farms. Many were only fifteen or sixteen years old. A few, in their late thirties, were veterans reenlisting. Even though the men were strangers, Deborah felt a strong sense of belonging to a group that shared the cause of liberty.

Some of the men no doubt enlisted only for the bounty money and army pay, irregular though it was reported to be. But all were committed to bearing arms against the common oppressor. The spirit of comradery and togetherness held for Deborah the quality of the happy times she shared with her ten adopted brothers on the farm. She had seen little of her four real brothers since she was almost five when her father had deserted the family and supposedly drowned at sea.

At the start of the march south from Worcester, Deborah suddenly became filled with fear, wanted to disappear from the face of the earth. As she later told Herman Mann, she felt like shrinking into nothing, "like a fly rolled up in the fold of a dark curtain." But within a few hours, the excitement all around her left no time for fear. This desire to vanish under conditions of terror was a characteristic reaction of almost everyone fighting in the war. But it was balanced for Deborah by her strong wish to help her country gain its freedom.

The fifty recruits became one hundred, then two hundred, then three hundred, swelling the ranks of the original group as they picked up men along the way. They crossed the Connecticut River, the fertilizing Nile of New England, at Lovejoy's Ferry, ten miles below Springfield. The march through Connecticut brought recruits from New Hampshire, Vermont and Rhode Island. The line of recruits grew, like waters flowing into the Connecticut River on its voyage to the sea.

Sometimes wives, sweethearts, parents and children would accompany the men on a whole day's march, separating only at nightfall to return home. One young woman had to be forcibly held back by her parents, not wanting to leave the man she loved. A youthful recruit stepped away at sunset from ranks he had just joined, obviously having second thoughts about leaving his village, as he kissed the dandelions growing by the side of the road.

Some of the men carried trumpets, drums and fifes. There was continuous music and singing, sometimes low and soft, sometimes loud and ringing so the very hills seemed to throb with melody.

The recruits slept on the hard ground with only the sky as their cover. Sometimes during the day Deborah staggered so with such weariness she broke ranks, reeled against the man to her right, then the one to her left, as though she had just polished off two rum flips. She wondered why the sergeant did not seem upset by her staggering. Then she noticed others staggered too.

When they crossed the Housatonic at New Milford, Deborah felt so weary she thought of throwing herself in the river. She would have done so, she later told Mann, had her mind been as ready to sink as her body. Her feet became blistered and the blisters broke but she gamely continued onward. Both she and the others waited eagerly for Sergeant Gambel to call the coveted "Halt!" which meant rest and sleep.

She wondered how she would be able to conceal her sex when she had to go to the toilet. But she resolved this problem simply. She observed that the men, when they felt the need to relieve themselves, wandered off, one by one, into the privacy of the woods. She did the same. If they ate in a tavern, they used the facilities there.

Fortunately for Deborah, they all slept in their clothes, as she had done in her wanderings through Massachusetts. If it rained hard, they sought a nearby tavern for the night. They did not bathe except to wash face and hands occasionally in streams along the way or at the taverns.

On the tenth day, just two days' march from West Point, they awoke to a pelting rain and very cold weather for the first week in June. But they marched all day, splashing through puddles, soaked to the skin and chilled to the bone. Deborah's once elegant suit and farm boots were caked with mud.

Early in the evening Sergeant Gambel called "Halt!" in front of a tavern. Deborah did not know if she had the strength even to stagger to the warmth of the burning logs at the far end of the room. She managed to reach the fireplace, then fell to the floor in a faint.

She regained consciousness to find a young, dark-haired woman leaning over her, trying to force a glass of wine between her lips, looking at her sympathetically. The young woman told her that many recruits fainted at this point in the long march.

Suddenly the woman took Deborah in her arms and stroked her forehead seductively. For the first time since she had stepped into a man's suit, Deborah was embarrassed, flustered. It had never occurred to her that a woman might believe her a strong, supple youth and be attracted to her.

She hastily raised herself from the floor, brushed herself off and thanked the young woman. The latter then offered her shelter for the night, saying Deborah could share the bed of her husband who owned the tavern and that she herself would sleep in the attic. Deborah quickly replied she had fully recovered and would remain with the recruits. She joined the men at the bar with great relief. They had not even noticed she had fainted.

The next day they neared the vicinity of West Point. The formerly sequestered farm girl felt a new kind of excitement as wagon after wagon now started to pass them, filled with military supplies and farm produce. They were bound for army headquarters across the river at New Windsor and the army supply depot at Fishkill.

The vital Fishkill fortifications, needed to protect the supplies, were under the command of Major General Baron Frederick William Augustus Von Steuben, a native of Germany and organizer and disciplinarian par excellence of the army. He had been responsible for turning a group of unreliable volunteers who had never marched a step in unison into well-trained and disciplined men.

The lengthy march, while replete with drudgery and fatigue, also fed Deborah's intelligence and quest for worldly knowledge as life on the farm never could. As she marched, she looked and learned, thrilled at new sights—the way she felt her father must have when he arrived in England. As the army marched over a mountain, she saw below the bustling town of Fishkill, filled with barracks, workshops and fortifications. It was barricaded partly by the fortifications, partly by the mountains.

They passed an army prison where she glimpsed captives in redcoat uniforms and others who, she was told, were Tories. They had been captured as part of a group that, along with Indians, had marched up the Mohawk River to Lake Ontario. There they had wantonly burned more than two hundred "rebel" homes and killed the owners, the horses and meat cattle as well as destroying one hundred thousand bushels of corn needed by the Continental Army.

The weary recruits now faced a twenty-mile march south to Peekskill, along the stagecoach road from Albany to White Plains. It was a route over mountains and through dark, heavy forests, a paradise for owls and bears, if not exhausted soldiers. Recent settlers laid claim to the land, except for the opening here and there of a cowpath.

They headed for King's Ferry, part of Verplanck's Point, six miles south of Peekskill. The ferry would take them across the Hudson River to Stony Point. This scenic crossing, one of the few along the Hudson River, was used by civilian ferries with sails, carrying farmers, travelers, and by army barges for the soldiers and recruits. Despite all the fortifications, the trip across the river proved a welcome break in the daily routine for Deborah, who fantasied herself for the moment at sea, like her father.

At this stage of the war General Washington's chief fear was that the British, who still held New York City, would attempt to capture the important army base at West Point and recapture outposts along the Hudson they once held.

Both sides of the ferry route, Verplanck's Point on the east and Stony Point on the west, under the command of General Anthony Wayne, were strongly fortified. They had been captured in the spring of 1779 by the British, whose eyes focused on West Point. The two points were retaken in bitter battles by the Continental troops.

Even earlier, in October, 1777, the British, attacking by land and by river, had captured Fort Montgomery and Fort Clinton, five miles below West Point. The naval expedition, under the command of Major General Sir Henry Clinton, was part of the British scheme to ascend the Hudson River and give relief to General Burgoyne. He was struggling against the Continental Army, under the command of Major General Horatio Gates, in an attempt to open a line of communication between Canada and New York by way of Lake Champlain and the Hudson. If successful, this would sever the eastern states from the middle states and starve the Continental Army, which depended on many of the colonies for its survival.

After the successful assault and destruction of the two forts, the elated Major General Clinton wanted to communicate with Burgoyne, then marching with his entire force toward Albany from Canada. General Clinton selected a confidential messenger, then called a spy, Daniel Taylor, and gave him a dispatch that informed Burgoyne, "Here we are and nothing between us but Gates. I sincerely hope this little success of ours may facilitate your operations."

The message had been written on a piece of tissue paper three inches square, then folded and encased in a silver pillbox the size of a cranberry, described by General Clinton as a "bullet." He gave it to Taylor with instructions to hand it only to General Burgoyne.

Taylor was ordered to swallow the "bullet" if captured by the Americans.

The American garrisons, under the command of General Clinton's cousin, Governor George Clinton, were dispersed throughout the mountains in that vicinity. Reaching a point about four miles west of New Windsor, General Clinton halted, established his headquarters at the house of a Mrs. Falls. He tried to collect his scattered troops so he could go to the defense of Kingston, toward which the victorious British were racing.

About noon on October 10 a man in a civilian suit was seen riding rapidly toward Governor Clinton's camp. The man approached a party of American soldiers clad in red coats they had removed from the few British soldiers captured when the two forts fell. The coats were in far better condition than those of the Americans, who needed them as protection against the cold weather. In answer to the horseback rider's inquiries, the soldiers told him their camp was under "Clinton's command."

The rider was Daniel Taylor and, confused by the similarity of names and seeing soldiers in red coats, he asked to see General Clinton, believing him to be Major General Sir Henry Clinton. (He thought the British had moved with such speed they had arrived in the area before him.)

Taylor was presented to Governor Clinton and in the confusion that followed, as Taylor learned his mistake, he was observed placing something in his mouth, then swallowing it. Governor Clinton ordered Dr. Moses Higby of the nearby town of Little Britain to give Taylor a powerful dose of tartar emetic. This brought forth the "bullet." Taylor was tried, convicted as a spy, sentenced to death. He was hanged from an apple tree almost in sight of the burning town of Kingston, which the British had reached and were reducing to ashes.

But now, Deborah learned, there were no redcoats nearer than

Westchester County to the south, then New York City. As the recruits approached King's Ferry, they met army officers on horseback who hailed them with cheerful greetings. An infantry battalion, accompanied by a small band, suddenly appeared on the road and escorted the soldiers to the river's brink at Verplanck's Point.

Deborah had never seen a river as wide or as blue as the Hudson. She later spoke of marveling at its beauty as she stood in awe on the army barge that crossed the river then eased into Stony Point. The latter received its name from the large rocks that jutted out of the water.

Stepping off the barge, the group started the thirteen-mile march to West Point along a stagecoach road that ran north and south on the west side of the river. The recruits enjoyed the sight of the Hudson to the right as they slowly climbed higher and higher up hills, then down into valleys where marshy inlets were banked by reeds for miles.

One long final climb with breathtaking views of mountains on both sides of the river brought the soldiers to the plateau that was West Point. It stretched about a mile long and a mile wide on a mighty cliff six hundred feet above the river.

The army rented the land from the Moore family; what had once been corn fields and cow pastures was now an impregnable series of forts, redoubts and smaller fortifications. They were set not only on the plateau but the mountain behind it. Cliffs fronted the river, facing those across the river on Constitution Island. West Point, Deborah realized, was a natural fortress, guardian of the vulnerable and valuable waterway below. This would be her new home.

She and her cohorts were excited to see cannon, brass and iron guns mounted on the five main forts and the redoubts flanking the forts. Filled with pride, they watched a number of flags, each bearing a constellation of thirteen stars, waving over the fortifications and ramparts. Some of the flags had been battered by storms and torn apart by lightning but still soared bravely aloft, to the everlasting glory of the Continental Army of which Deborah was now a part. She felt as if her dream of fighting for her country's freedom was starting to come true.

Fort Clinton, named after the American general, sat on the crest of the point at the northern tip. Looking north at the spectacular view, Deborah was captivated by its beauty. The Hudson River, in its 250-mile sweep from the Canadian border to the harbor of New York City, sliced a narrow, twisting gorge through the Hudson Highlands. Formed of a strip of ancient granite, the Highland mountains ran east and west of the river. They stood 50 miles north of New York City, at that time a night's sail away. Steep green precipices banked the river's 15-mile passage through the rugged heights.

In 1782, the spot where the Hudson River met the Highlands was the key to the continent. The British sought it desperately in their final attempt to defeat the Continental Army. West Point, called "the Gibraltar of America" because of the fortification and protection of its high cliffs, commanded a clear view south to the enemy. The river at that point was 165 feet deep, the distance across only 1400 feet.

In the area of this "west point," as it was called for decades, the white man had displaced the original Indian settlers—the Algonquins, the Mohicans, the Tappans, the Mincees and the Manhattans. As Deborah arrived, there remained no visual reminder of the Indians. The only sign of habitation was an occasional farmhouse.

On the point, just southwest of Fort Clinton, Fort Putnam stood on a mountain, cannons lining the three redoubts above it. Fort Webb lay directly south. Still further south stood Fort

Wyllys, also lined with artillery. Below it, Fort Meigs protected the southernmost part of the point.

This military fortress, still uncompleted, had taken three years of army labor and three million dollars to construct under the direction of Major Peter Charles l'Enfant and Thaddeus Kosciusko, of the corps of engineers. Soldiers had cut down the plentiful trees nearby to make huts for the officers, who slept in them two apiece. The enlisted men had tents, usually five to eight in a "common" tent. On marches they built brush shelters in the outdoors against rain and cold.

The fortress was protected by fifteen hundred soldiers, of whom Deborah was now one. They understood that its fall to the British would be disastrous to the patriot cause, stopping all trade between New England and the central and southern states. Loss of control of the Hudson River would wipe out needed army resources from the river valley. Flour, lumber and grain came from lands bordering the river, fish from the river, draft horses for the military from regions near Albany, uniforms for soldiers made from the wool of Massachusetts and cattle from the New England states.

Deborah recalled that only two years before one of the most terrifying dramas of the war took place. Major General Benedict Arnold, one of the war's heroes, arrived on August 5, 1780 to take command of the fortress, succeeding General Robert Howe. General Arnold had conspired with Major John André, Adjutant-general of the British Army, to turn West Point and all its troops and supplies over to the British.

Major André, captured by chance near Tarrytown as he tried to get through to the British lines in New York, carried papers revealing the plot. A Tory messenger brought General Arnold the news of Major André's capture. Leaving his wife and young son behind, General Arnold fled by barge to the fourteen-gun sloop, the *H.M.S. Vulture,* anchored to the south near Dobbs Ferry.

When General Washington, staying overnight at the Robinson House just across the river at Fort Constitution, heard of the treachery, he is reported to have asked sadly, "Who do we have now that we can trust?" The main fort, Fort Arnold, was promptly renamed Fort Clinton. Major André was executed but General Arnold escaped.

Deborah, reading of this horror in the quiet of Middleborough, now saw with her own eyes where it took place. She felt exuberant, truly part of the war.

Deborah was assigned to a tent she would share with six other soldiers, members of a company grouped together in two long rows of tents that stood southwest of Fort Clinton. The soldiers slept on wooden bunks with mattresses consisting of crocus, a yellow-colored material used as bed linen. The straw in the mattress was changed weekly.

A large hole in the center of each tent floor served as a fireplace, logs placed in them when the weather was cold. The tent's foundation was a nest of pine branches and leaves that kept the tent dry and warm. Barracks' masters supervised the distribution of crocus, straw, firewood and iron pots for cooking. If an ambitious group of soldiers wanted a more elegant home away from home, they could build their own wooden or stone hut.

Deborah shared a bed at times with another soldier but this did not upset her. When she boarded out in Middleborough, she often shared a bed with a woman servant. But now, because her bunkmate was a man, she placed her body at first precariously on the edge of her side of the bunk. She also may have moved as far away from the soldier as possible because this was the first time she slept close to a man and was afraid she might be attracted to him. But soon she became accustomed to sharing the bunk; both occupants felt so fatigued by night they were totally unaware of their bed partner.

Lining up to receive her military gear, Deborah was pleased to receive a French musket, or Charleville firelock. This was lighter and smaller than the American musket, intended as a weapon for light infantrymen, who had to be more mobile than the ordinary foot troops. The French, who supplied much of the army's military equipment, had standardized at caliber .70 the pistols, muskets and fusils used by company grade officers. This simplified the supply of ammunition.

Deborah also was given thirty cartridges and a cartouche cartridge box with sling, which she proudly carried on her left shoulder. She wore her bayonet and scabbard either on her waist belt or slung over her right shoulder.

For marches, her equipment consisted of a wooden canteen, worn above her left waist and slung over her right shoulder on top of her haversack. The haversack was a coarse white linen pack that carried rations. She wore this over her right shoulder at an angle on her back. It contained extra clothing, personal items like toothbrush, mirror, handkerchiefs, writing items, a Bible and in the winter a five-by-seven-foot heavy woolen blanket.

Her uniform, issued by the quartermaster general, included a deep blue regimental, or outer linen coat. She was pleased that the blue of her coat highlighted the tinctured blue in her eyes. The coat was faced white on its cuffs, lapels and collar, with a white lining and blue hearts for reinforcements on each of the regimental coat tails. Waistcoats and overalls were made of white linen. The overalls were long trousers cut snug to the leg. Shaped to cover her ankles and shoe tops like a gaiter, they were flattering to her long, slender limbs. Properly fitted, they provided freedom of action and more protection than the knee breeches and stockings worn earlier in the war. Wool stockings and black leather stout boots, made straight, no right or left, square-toed with shoe buckles, completed the uniform except for the light infantry cap.

Special to the light infantry, this cap was decorated by the "variegated cockade"—the "union cockade"—worn by American troops. It combined the United States black cockade with the French white. Like a rosette, it was worn on one side of the cap. On the other side rose a black plume, its upper half red-tipped, brought from France by Lafayette for the light infantry. Deborah must have felt a secret pleasure wearing, in the disguise of a soldier, a cap attractive enough to be worn by the beautiful women of Boston.

Officers wore beaver tricorn hats and provided their own uniforms. Soldiers were furnished uniforms but had to reimburse the army out of their pay, if and when they were fortunate enough to receive any.

The change from a civilian suit into her uniform caused Deborah a moment of anxiety. She kept her eyes on the ground, not daring to look at the men, though it would have been nothing new for her to see a male body. Many times she had watched one of the ten Thomas boys race naked through the rooms on a summer's night, bent for the outhouse, disregarding his mother's command to put on breeches. She also had helped bathe and diaper the younger boys after they were born. Even with her Puritan upbringing she was not shocked to fasten her eyes on that precious appendage denied women that seemed to give men such special status.

Thus it was not the idea of seeing men nude that made her anxious but the fear that her own body would be exposed and her disguise ripped away. But she slowly took off her civilian suit, quickly slipped on the uniform. She adroitly kept herself covered so as not to reveal her feminine form. She stepped out of the heavy, mud-covered farm boots and, with relief, threw them on the refuse pile.

As she stood in the white overalls, shirt, waistcoat and regimental coat, getting the feel of the uniform of the Continental Army, she felt the thrill of being one woman alone among fifteen hundred men—she who had suffered the indignity at age four-and-a-half of being turned down by the Continental Navy. Deborah enjoyed a feeling of naturalness in spite of the unnaturalness of war. Sometimes she had worn one of the older Thomas boys' hand-me-down shirts or breeches when she went fishing with them for trout in the swift-running streams, or when they hunted turkey and rabbit in the woods. This current masculine attire did not feel strange.

Deborah's eyes kept searching apprehensively throughout the camp for sight of one of the ten Thomas boys—most of whom had enlisted—or for one of her brothers. Would they give her away if she found them? It was with relief, as well as sadness, that she could not discover one familiar face. Either they lived in smaller camps in other parts of the nation, had died on the battlefield or of one of the many diseases that swept through the camps.

In the morning, Deborah's company was ordered to march to the green. There they assembled to meet Sergeant Calvin Munn. He was selected to give them "the first rudiments of discipline," a discipline Deborah had proved she did not need. Sergeants wore white shoulder knots of worsted on each shoulder, corporals wore only one knot on the right shoulder.

The next day the company was instructed in drilling and firing. They received and were ordered to learn every word of the regulations in the manual of arms, an impressive booklet written by General Baron Von Steuben.

In the mess hall they ate a fare of salt beef, green peas, bread, butter and molasses. The soldiers usually were so hungry they would have eaten wood shavings. Deborah was eager to learn more about the army and that night in the tent, using a candle in a tin lantern, she studied the manual of arms. Among other instructions, it told how to load and fire a musket, also called a firelock. The manual informed her of the procedure on marches, the primary duties of a soldier and gave a description of the various ranks.

The first few nights she was kept awake by the snores, wheezes and grunts around her as she tossed from side to side on the straw pallet. But after a while, exhausted, she sank into deep, untroubled sleep. The men slept in their uniforms after removing the regimental coat and waistcoat. They seemed to consider their shirt, breeches and often their socks as underwear, since they wore no other. She was grateful for this custom as it spared her the need to disrobe before them, greatly reducing her chances of discovery.

The sound of a drum roll beating reveille and the first rays of dawn awakened her. The men sighed, groaned and reluctantly slipped on shoes and waistcoats as they complained of having to rise so early. But Deborah felt the excitement of facing the new day, thankful she had been trained by Mr. and Mrs. Benjamin Thomas to feed the chickens and escort the cows to pasture as the sun rose.

They assembled on the green for roll call. She answered "Here!" without hesitation, loud and clear, when the name Robert Shurtliff was called.

In the next few days Sergeant Munn earned his pay, drilling the recruits until they felt at home with musket and bayonet. Most of the men were fairly adept at handling a musket since they, like Deborah, had hunted animals on their farms.

The musket, which the men called their "piece," could fire only two musket balls a minute, three at the most, because of the time it took to load a musket ball. There were many movements to the loading: Deborah first had to remove the musket from her shoulder, then reach into the cartouche for the cartridge. With her teeth she tore open the paper enclosing the cartridge and poured the powder into a pan. She then wheeled the musket over, dropped in the powder and the musket ball. Next she took the ramrod from the pipes underneath the gun barrel and pushed the powder and ball all the way down the barrel so it would not backfire. Finally she had to take out the ramrod, place it back in the pipes. Then she brought the musket up, cocked it and waited for the officer's command, "Fire!"

Each firing had to be in unison with those of the other soldiers in the company so it would be more effective attacking the enemy. This was not difficult for Deborah, as she had hunted in coopera-tion with the ten Thomas brothers.

She also learned how to swing a bayonet so she could wound or kill an enemy at close quarters. Brought up on the philosophy of the Bible, "Revenge is mine, saith the Lord," it was difficult for her at first to think of plunging a bayonet into a human body, even an enemy. For a woman especially, to kill a man would be terrify-ing but, as she informed Mann, when a redcoat or Tory shot at her or raised a saber against her, she thought only of saving her life. It never occurred to her that on an unconscious level, as we shall later see through her famous nightmare, with every plunge of the bayonet she was killing the father who had deserted her. She now considered herself a warrior, wore a martial plume and a sheathless cutlass. She reassured herself she had made it thus far without giving herself away and would make it *all* the way.

Because of the shortage of volunteers, a company, authorized at 180 men, was likely to be composed of only 60 to 70 privates. The regimental strength on paper was 750 soldiers of all ranks. A brigade, usually 4 to 8 men, now consisted only of 4 to 6. There was 1 corporal for every 10 men, 1 sergeant for every 2 corporals, and 4 sergeants to a company.

As on the march, one of Deborah's chief concerns was how she would manage her toilet necessities and prevent discovery of her sex. The regimental outhouses or latrines consisted of lone planks raised a foot from the earth, each with a series of round holes through which cupfuls of lime were tossed frequently to dispel odors.

Deborah noticed that some of the men preferred to wander into the woods rather than use the latrines and she did the same if she had to relieve herself during the day. At night usually there was no one in the latrines, or if there was it was too dark to see very clearly. As a rule anyone who wandered in was too sleepy to care about anything but relieving himself and staggering back to his straw pallet.

The men washed their faces and hands in basins of water carried in leather buckets from the springs behind the barracks. When someone took a bath, usually only when ordered by a sergeant, he filled a barrel with water or swam in the Hudson. Deborah cleansed herself in the dark to avoid bathing publicly in the barrels or river during this very warm weather. Luckily, no sergeant gave her orders to bathe "at once." Under such circumstances much of her thinking and daily routines became determined by the need to avoid exposure of her sex.

The staple diet was salt pork or salt beef and bread. Fish, chicken, turkeys and deer were often served. Many provisions were scarce because of inflated prices. Army prices were regulated: turkeys sold for $3.00, geese, $2.00, chickens, $.50, potatoes, $1.37 a bushel, butter, $1.37 a tub, brown sugar, $2.00 a pound and a loaf of bread, $1.00 a pound. The army often bartered with the farmers, offering salt, a preservative desperately needed, instead of the highly inflated, almost worthless Continental currency.

The soldiers were supposed to get a daily ration but often

transportation difficulties and the scarcity of food made this impossible. The weekly ration consisted of one pound of bread or
flour, a quarter pound of beef and a half pound of salt pork, one pint
of milk, one gill (a quarter of a pint) of peas or beans, six ounces of
butter, one pound of common soap for six men, and half a pint of
vinegar per man. Sometimes the army procured hogs, potatoes,
bacon—but no lamb, as it was against the law to kill sheep,
needed for wool.

The officers ate in a formal mess hall at the Moore House, a large
farm north of the commandant's quarters. The rank and file ate
three times a day in shifts in their mess hall. When no fighting
took place there seemed little to do but report each morning for
drill, take part in the grand parade in the afternoon, and eat.
Informal messes were set up outside the tents of most companies.

Soldiers took turns as chef or delegated one soldier, if he possessed special culinary skill, to be permanent chef. The company
had its own iron and copper pots and frying pans, which it carried
on marches. The men would forage for berries or wild game in the
woods or fish in the streams and the Hudson River. (Major General
Baron Von Steuben once reported seeing a whale in the Hudson but
it proved only a very large eel.)

Packet boats plied daily between West Point and Newburgh
carrying orders from General Washington, who kept in close touch
with his officers at the military fortress. He had just made the
recommendation that the troops plant "regimental gardens, for the
purpose of raising greens and vegetables for their own use." He
suggested "in order to collect a sufficient quantity of seeds, commanding officers of regiments will give passes to as many trusty
soldiers as they may judge necessary to go into the country and to
be absent not exceeding ten days."

He added, "The General hopes he shall see a suitable attention
bestowed on an article which will contribute so much to the

comfort and health of the troops. He even flatters himself it will become a matter of amusement and of emulation."

Deborah felt at home as she planted peas, beans, turnips and later helped harvest the crop. Each officer's hut had its kitchen garden. The quartermaster general advertised in local newspapers for seeds and flourishing vegetable gardens bloomed all over the fortress. The army had learned, after the tragic lesson at Valley Forge where thousands of men had died of scurvy, that lack of vegetables caused this disease.

The soldiers were also given daily rations of one gill of rum to keep up their spirits. This small amount was not enough for many. They traded their bread or salt rations with other soldiers for the liquor ration or bought it from camp peddlers or sutlers. This practice led General Washington to issue the order that each soldier be placed on a liquor roll and the amount of rum consumed daily be recorded. Those who drank too much were struck off the rolls, forfeiting their rations. General Washington also ordered sergeants to mix water with the rum ration to prevent "the evil practice of swallowing the whole ration of liquor in a single draught."

Soldiers were not the only ones at this time to have a thirst for rum. Before the War of Independence each colonist, women and children included, downed twenty-four pints of rum per year. Rum soothed the spirits of exhausted pioneers eking out their living from primitive, uncultivated land. In fact some insisted it was not the Boston Tea Party that caused the American Revolution but the British tax on molasses (from which rum is made) that kindled the spark responsible for the final schism between Britain and the Colonies.

Soldiers who did not drink could trade their liquor rations for vegetables or any article needed. Deborah did not wish to drink, fearing the rum might loosen her tongue as it once did in the near past at her local tavern, and she would reveal she was a woman. She traded her daily liquor ration for paper, quills and ink brought from the army depots at Fishkill.

She also used her ration to buy linen cloth for use once a month, to protect herself during menstruation, preventing the blood from staining her white breeches. When she learned she had the option of trading her liquor ration for whatever goods she needed, she exchanged it for these pieces of linen cloth, used by the men as towels. She also could buy linen from women at the post who did the laundry and other housekeeping tasks.

Deborah kept the cloth hidden under her burlap mattress or in her haversack until needed. She never allowed menstrual cramps to keep her from carrying out patrol duties or collecting firewood. When she knew she would be spending several days on a march and expected the flow of blood along the way, she wore a linen strip as safeguard, carrying an extra supply in her haversack. To get rid of the incriminating blood-soaked strip, she would steal into the woods at night and bury it in soft loam. If a man were awake and saw her wander off, he would assume she was relieving herself behind a tree.

Living with the soldiers was an experience in democracy for Deborah, one drastically different from the simple society of Middleborough where almost everyone was a farmer and lived according to strict religious and moral creeds. Some of the men ate as if they had never seen a pewter spoon, knife or fork. A large number chewed tobacco all day, spitting it at will. There were men who mangled the King's English, as though they had never read the Bible. Many cursed freely.

General Washington sent orders to all Brigades in 1777, saying, "Decency and good breeding, as well as morality and religion, dictate that profane swearing ought to be discouraged and rendered disreputable. The General flatters himself a single hint will be sufficient on this subject to the troops whose distinguishing characteristic has ever been the most prompt and cheerful obedience not only to the orders but to the recommendations of the General commanding."

But now the general's "single hint" was not enough. Five years later he stated his feelings were "continually wounded by the oaths and imprecations of the soldiers whenever I am in hearing of them. The name of that Being from whose bountiful goodness we are permitted to exist and enjoy the comforts of life, is incessantly imprecated and profaned in a manner so wanton as it is shocking." He requested officers of every rank to use their influence and authority "to check a vice which is as unprofitable as it is wicked and shameful."

That order too might just as well never have been sent. The cursing either took the name of the Lord in vain or referred in some way to the devil.

Deborah always tried to be pleasant to her comrades but never allowed herself to get close to anyone. She thought there would be less chance to give herself away if she kept to herself. She tried not to show embarrassment when the men spoke of their sexual desires for, and experiences with, camp followers. She later told Herman Mann that as she listened to the men describe their sexual activities, she wondered how often it was fancy rather than fact.

The need to keep her feminine sex secret consumed valuable time in Deborah's life. At an age when it was normal for unattached young women to dream of lovers she had to stay aloof from men to hide her precious secret—possibly also to avoid awakening her sexual desire which, at this point, could not be consummated in marriage.

Unlike headquarters at New Windsor where troops were supplied under an overall contract that took care of "the moving army," few women lived on the post. Wives of the officers and civilian contractors completing construction work or supplying provisions to West Point made up the contingent.

A large number of women refugees from New York City, fleeing the British, lived in New Windsor and Newburgh. Another group in Fishkill was employed by the quartermaster general to make clothing and cartridges for the army. The camp followers were chiefly destitute women who did not want, or found it impossible to get work. They camped as near as they could to the soldiers, their breadwinners.

Deborah later told Mann she was shocked to see women fall to such degradation. She thought it ironic that were she to be discovered, she would be censured more for wielding a gun and bayonet in defense of her country than "these soldiers' trulls" who served the men sexually.

The men seemed without question to accept Deborah as one of them. At times they taunted her, but kindly, calling her "Molly" and "smock-face," referring to her lack of a beard, implying she was the age of a boy-child dressed in a smock. An older soldier said to her one night, "Wait until you've smelt a little gunfire and tasted soldier's food a few years. You'll go home with a beard and whiskers as large as a brush-heap." The men undoubtedly thought her a shy youngster, homesick, as many of them were.

It was an ever-present hazard living among young men, needing to safeguard each moment against their finding out she was a woman. It added to the thrill but at the same time caused her to exist in perpetual fear that, should anyone discover the truth, she might be court-martialed, even sentenced to be shot. Of this she was sure. She believed death would be her punishment for deceiving the Continental Army.

When not drilling or eating or sleeping, the men played a game called whisk or gambled with three dice, made of lead, musket balls or wood. They also threw horseshoes or knives in a game of mumblety-peg or sat thoughtfully smoking long-stemmed clay pipes to keep mosquitoes away. They read newspapers several weeks old or whittled decorative wood objects. Sometimes they made spiked candle holders to be driven into posts for night use or fashioned bone combs for getting lice out of their hair. They also designed ice creepers for cutting snow and ice in winter or went sightseeing, hiking up the steep Storm King Mountain north of the point.

In the evening the men indulged in horseplay, practical jokes on the unsuspecting. They also sang English ballads and drinking songs to the accompaniment of fifes and Jews harps. There often was heard the sound of music for each regiment had its drummer and fifer. An inspector of music regulated the beat on special occasions such as grand parades.

To her regret, Deborah arrived at West Point one week too late to take part in the singular celebration honoring the birth of the dauphin, the French crown prince. An order for a *feu de joie*, or fire of joy, was given by General Washington. Ten blank cartridges were issued to each musketman as every field piece was fired simultaneously. A three-cannon salute, whose reverberations rang from cliff to cliff, opened and closed the ceremony.

General Washington and his wife Martha arrived in his special barge, rowed down from his Newburgh headquarters to take part in the banquet for five hundred officers and their wives. The soldiers each received an extra gill of rum which they drank as they watched the officers dance in a newly constructed colonnade. Fireworks shooting over the Hudson were part of the festivities.

Each night Deborah wrote briefly of the day's happenings in a small notebook she ordered from Fishkill. Some of the men who could not write, seeing her scribble away, begged her to send a few lines for them to a wife, a sweetheart, a mother.

She wrote many a mother but never her own, yearning to but not daring. She feared her mother might give away her secret, fearful for her daughter's life in such a dangerous situation. Her mother would never understand what had driven her daughter to place herself in such a precarious, unorthodox role.

THE FIRST
BATTLE

Because Deborah was tall and sturdy, agile and a fine marksman, she was assigned to a special group in the Light Infantry Division called the rangers. The light infantry—one company picked from each continental infantry regiment—was the elite of the Continental Army. During a special campaign they were detached from their parent regiments for special missions and regrouped into provisional light infantry battalions after the British custom.

The assignment was a triumph for Deborah. Not only had she accomplished the almost impossible feat of getting herself accepted into a man's army but she functioned so successfully as a soldier that her superior officers accepted her as an esteemed member of the armed forces.

Deborah's division was led by Captain George Webb. It was part of the First Brigade, commanded by General John Paterson. All the brigades were under the command of Major General Henry Knox, commandant of West Point, who had been a bookseller in Boston before the war.

The missions of the rangers, who went out on small scouting parties, included spying on enemy movements and bringing back intelligence information, as well as capturing Tories.

On the tenth day after Deborah arrived, just as the month of June started, she was ordered to draw four days' provisions for a special march. The rangers planned to embark on a scouting mission south to Harlem, just below King's Bridge, eight miles from New York City. They would march through neutral territory, an area of fifty miles of rich, fertile land between the American fortifications at Peekskill and British headquarters in Manhattan.

The British domain extended just outside New York City to King's Bridge and West Farms on the Bronx River. This territory had been the scene of violence and lawlessness. If Deborah or any other ranger were captured by Tories or redcoats they would be considered within the British lines and hung as spies. It was with some terror as well as pride that Deborah accepted her prestigious assignment.

General Washington had sent an order to the officers instructing them that "the corps of Light Infantry encamp forthwith upon the high ground in front of Peekskill," for the purpose of ridding the neutral territory of British spies, loyalists and Tories. Companies of loyalist militia, some under the command of redcoats, were making forays on patriot farms. Individual loyalists intercepted the

mails, scouted and spied on the continental troops, even captured
and killed small detachments of patriot soldiers.

A particularly vicious group of Tories, chiefly descendants of old
Dutch settlers, were known as the Westchester Light Horse Battalion. Stationed at Morrisania, near Long Island Sound, they were
under the command of Colonel James DeLancey. They raided
patriot homes, stole food for British troops, raped women, looted
possessions and burned down houses. Such Tories were called
"damned cowboys" and patriots opposing them, "skinners."

New York, the most loyal to the British crown of the northern
colonies, was the stronghold of the Tories. Of the state's 182,000
inhabitants, nearly half were supposed to be loyalists. They were
chiefly the large landowners who traced their ancestry to the
original Dutch settlers, or descendants of the favorites of the
British Duke of York, who had brashly marched into New Amster-
dam one day in 1664, seized it from the Dutch without firing a
shot, and renamed it in his honor.

Along with about forty other rangers, Deborah packed her
haversack with rations of cold meat, peas, bread and filled her
canteen with water. Their particular mission was to slip as far as
possible behind enemy lines and return with a report of troop
movements or new fortifications.

The brave scouting party marched to Stony Point where they
were rowed by army barge to Verplanck's Point, reversing the route
by which Deborah had arrived at West Point. Then they walked
along trails over the hills to Tarrytown, about fifteen miles south,
camping there overnight. A veteran of long marches by now,
Deborah no longer experienced the dreadful fatigue of her first
journey south. The June weather was mild and the soldiers slept on
the ground, using their haversacks as pillows. If Deborah slept
fitfully, it was caused more by the anxiety of her new mission than
by physical discomfort. In the morning, the party divided in half

to cover a wider territory, agreeing to meet that night in White Plains, just southeast of Tarrytown.

Deborah's group made its way south, staying well off the main road. Spotting three British sentinels, they crept through the woods until they reached Harlem, just inside the British lines. There they were able to note the numbers and military strength of enemy troops, thus accomplishing their mission. Then, as had been arranged, they turned back to White Plains to meet the other half of the scouting party.

They reverently crossed the fields in White Plains that had been the scene of battles on October 28, 29, 1776. Deborah found herself extremely moved visiting this site of early American heroism. She later told Herman Mann she touched some of the earth with her toes, visualizing the clash of arms between the British and Continental Army. She rolled a special musket ball in poignant memory of the fallen patriots, which she saved.

Her group spent the night encamped in White Plains. In the morning, after a breakfast of bread, bacon and coffee cooked over a fire by the appointed chef (who had brought along a few pots and pans), they marched up a trail to Tarrytown.

Suddenly a volley of musket balls whizzed over Deborah's head. One musket ball struck a pine tree behind her. She whirled around to see a group of men on horseback, led by two redcoats who had appeared from behind a hill. Before her sergeant had time to order "Fire!", the attackers let loose a second round. One musket ball ripped through her hat. The red-tipped plume fell at her feet like the shattered mast of a ship. Deborah put aside her terror and continued the battle.

To the sergeant's order of "Fire!", in unison with the rest of her company she was able to aim, fire and reload. A number of enemy horses and riders fell to the ground. The Tories rallied, flanked by a large phalanx of armed loyalists on foot, fired again.

The man to her left was struck in the chest by a musket ball and dropped to the ground, his blood spurting on her breeches. The sergeant now ordered "Retreat!" With mixed feelings she followed him into the safety of nearby woods.

Deborah raced on foot behind the sergeant as the Tories pursued on horseback, firing as they galloped by. She heard several soldiers scream as they were struck by musket balls, saw fallen men thrashing around in their own blood.

There came a sound like a sudden gust of wind. A second bullet ripped through the side sleeve of her coat, tearing a hole in it. Then at once there arose a tumult of neighing horses, shouts of confusion, screams of pain, the smoke of gunpowder and the sight of redcoats fleeing in all directions.

Suddenly, gratefully, she became aware the ranks of the patriot soldiers had increased. Her besieged company had received three platoons of reinforcements from the Tarrytown post, which had raced to the rescue on hearing gunfire. They poured a barrage of musket balls into the Tories, killing a number of them. The rest turned and fled.

When the shots ceased, Deborah learned the enemy had been part of Colonel Delancey's dreaded Westchester battalion. The rescuing regiment was led by Colonel Ebenezer Sproat who, at six feet, four inches, was one of the tallest men in the army. She recognized him as a resident of Middleborough, owner of Sproat Tavern. It seemed as though some savior suddenly had been sent from her hometown. Although she had seen the colonel at the tavern where she drank an occasional glass of beer, he showed no signs of recognizing her. The pale, well-groomed young woman he had known in Middleborough was now somewhat aged by army hardships and attired in a soldier's uniform. She was smeared with gunpowder and perspiration rolled down her grimy face.

Deborah felt exhausted, hot and thirsty. When she reached the

Tarrytown post she eagerly drank almost a quart of ice water. A few hours later, she suffered such painful cramps she vowed never again to gulp ice water after battle.

She sadly watched her company bury its dead including three men she knew—John Beebe, Noble Sperin and James Battles. Her grief, as Shakespeare put it, made "old woes new" and brought back memories of dear ones temporarily lost to her. It reopened the deepest wound of all, the loss of her beloved father.

She felt relief her name was not among those of the heroic but dead soldiers. This was her baptism in battle—at moments she had thought it would be her first and last. She could think only of how savage it was to kill to be free. She thought of war as waged by untamed animals, not rational human beings. It had a ferocity that gave lie to all pretentions of humanity.

There appeared no other way at this time in history to gain freedom from tyranny. Maybe such senseless slaughter would end when men could talk over their differences and reach a compromise, caring enough about each other to give up slaughter. But since this was not yet the way of the world, though Deborah believed herself on the side of right, she had to fight in the world's ferocious fashion of conquering and killing the enemy.

Whatever her fears, her acts would be exemplary. She would defend herself to the death. After all, she had grown up with the Sampson coat of arms, which held "Disgrace is worse than death!" She had joined the patriot army and would not be thought a coward. That, to her, was more despicable than dying. She wanted to be as courageous as the bravest of men.

The world would never know Robert Shurtliff was a woman but she did not care. It was enough she knew in her own heart she would always act with a calm sort of courage.

THE BLOODY
WOUNDS

A few weeks after the Tory assault, a sergeant in Deborah's company praised her for her bravery in battle. He asked if she wished to volunteer with him for what the army called "a special mission to retaliate on the enemy."

Pleased at the growing recognition of her courage, she told him she would gladly be a volunteer. She despised the Tories, who played a *triple* double-dealing game of hunter, spy and traitor. She felt she would rather capture one Tory than five regular British grenadiers.

The sergeant explained they had to get approval for the special mission from the commander of the regiment. They walked to the quarters of Colonel Henry Jackson. He had succeeded Colonel Shepard, promoted to brigadier general, as the new commander of the Fourth Massachusetts Regiment. Colonel Jackson, a native of Boston, had fought in the Battle of Rhode Island. Though unrelenting in the discipline and decorum of his regiment, he had a naturalness and warmth that endeared him to his men.

Colonel Jackson looked at them skeptically after the sergeant explained why they were there, Deborah later told Mann. He then warned, "You two will be killed on such a mission and I have no men to spare."

"We'll get others to volunteer, sir," said the sergeant.

"If you can persuade twenty-eight other men to join you, you can go on the mission," the colonel agreed.

Deborah and the sergeant managed to round up the twenty-eight men and the next day set off with excitement for the neutral territory. They reached Vonhoite, near East Chester, without seeing a single Tory. There they patiently lay in ambush waiting to trap the enemy in the act of plundering patriot residents. As she crouched behind a tree, eyes and ears alert, Deborah mused how the slightest rustling of a leaf, even the whisper of the wind, could tell of danger.

The party saw two boys carrying a load of provisions to a cave in the woods. The sergeant who had organized the scouting party asked one of the boys, "What are you doing?"

"We're hiding food the Tories stole," said the loyalist sympathizer. "They left to get some Yankees who have been sniping at them but they're coming back for the food."

"We're Tories, too," lied the crafty sergeant. "Let's see what you've got."

The naive youngsters led them inside the cave. It was stacked with packages of bacon, butter, cheese, and jars of honey—far better fare than their own. In great spirits, the soldiers put down their muskets and haversacks. They ate heartily, then filled the haversacks with extra rations.

As they left the cave, the sergeant confessed, "Thanks a lot for the meal. We're from the rebel army."

The cave echoed with the outraged cries of the boys, who screamed as if they had fallen into the hands of bandits. One of them warned, "The Tories will return and they'll kill you when we tell them what you did!"

The sergeant, undaunted, snapped, "You better head home if you want to live." The boys ran off.

The scouting party decided to hide in the woods near the cave and trap the returning Tories. It was now dark. Stationing sentinels to wake them when the Tories approached, the weary soldiers lay down to sleep. Deborah had dozed for several hours, she judged, when she was awakened by a sentinel shaking her shoulders. She and the others stealthily took up their muskets, crept in the blackness to the cave. There they saw about forty Tories, most of them on horseback, all armed.

"Fire!" ordered the sergeant and they fired in unison at the Tories, taking them by surprise in the starlight. Several fell wounded from their horses. Others returned the fire as they retreated into the woods.

Suddenly Deborah saw a Tory officer who had lost his horse coming at her, his arm raised in the air, his hand gripping a saber. Remembering weeks of training, she threw her weight against the saber arm, diverting to her forehead a blow that would have slashed her throat. She felt a sharp crack against her head, for a moment saw stars.

Then, furious, she struck with all her might at the man, who was slight and smaller than she, hitting him over the head with her musket. He fell unconscious to the ground.

Even though her head throbbed, she ran toward a horse that had lost its rider. She hurled herself up on the saddle and with several other soldiers who also had mounted horses, she pursued the enemy in the dark.

They caught up with several Tories who had halted their horses in front of a large swamp. The Tories saw them approach, wheeled their horses and dashed into the woods to the right and left of the swamp, firing as they fled.

Deborah suddenly felt a sharp pain inside her left thigh, as though it had been pierced by fire. At the same time, a liquid warmer and thicker than perspiration from the hot night poured down the left side of her neck. With horror, she raised her hand to the site of the saber wound. When she drew it away she saw it was covered with blood.

She doggedly rode back to the rest of the scouting party who had remained at the cave. Drawing her horse to a halt, she dismounted, but discovered she was too weak to walk. Her left leg seemed paralyzed. She stared down at her boot, saw blood spilling out of it. Just below the groin, her breeches were torn. In the final firing by the Tories, a musket ball had ripped into the inside of her thigh.

With reluctance, Deborah called out to the sergeant who had asked her to volunteer for the mission, "I can't walk. I think I've been shot." She pointed to her bloody breeches.

He immediately replied, "I'm taking you to the French hospital. It's the nearest." A French field station had been set up at Crompound, where the French Army encamped.

She felt thirsty, always the symptom after battle, and asked quietly, "Could I have some water?"

The sergeant put his canteen to her lips. As she drank, she thought this emergency might be her undoing. She had no way to protect herself from being stripped of her clothes in the hospital. A true child of the Sampsons, she remembered their coat of arms, "Death is better than disgrace." She knew she had to fight with all her strength against such exposure, even if she had to risk death from an infected wound. She would stay behind in the woods resting on a bed of moss until either she recovered, with the help of God, or she died.

She told the sergeant, "I'm dying. Don't waste time on me. Leave me here."

But he would not listen. With the help of two other soldiers he lifted her, bloody from head to toe, onto a horse. (Deborah later told Mann she thought she must have looked like a piece of butchered meat.) Then the sergeant threw himself up behind her to hold her steady.

They galloped to the field hospital, several miles away. She winced each time she was jounced on the rutted road, as blood dripped from her head and leg. The dark blue night sky turned rose red in the dawn. She thought of killing herself before they discovered the truth about her sex and killed her. She looked at her musket holstered to the saddle, wondered how she might manage to maneuver the musket into position to shoot herself before arriving at the field station. But she realized with anguish that it would have been impossible to do so without the sergeant noticing her movements.

At the field hospital, the sergeant lifted her off the horse and with the help of other soldiers carried her inside and sat her on a chair. Three other wounded had been transported on horses.

A young French surgeon walked over to Deborah, looked at her bloody uniform and asked in broken English but a cheerful humane voice, "How you lose so much blood at this early hour?"

"Just a scrape," she responded.

"Be any bone broken?" he asked.

"I don't think so," she said.

He sympathetically offered her a large glass of wine to serve as anesthetic. Then he wiped the blood from her head wound and disinfected it with rum. She did not flinch though stabs of fire ran through her head. He rubbed a soothing salve on the wound, then bandaged it.

She asked for a second glass of wine, thinking she would need it. She was determined to remove the musket ball by herself, even though she had never even taken a splinter from her body.

The surgeon asked, "You have other wounds?"

"No," she lied.

He did not accept her lie. He said, "My lad, your boot say you tell fib," as he pointed to the blood oozing from it.

He gently took off her left boot and stocking, washed away the blood up to her knee. She thanked him. He suggested she go into an adjoining room and take off her bloody uniform.

Reenergized by the wine, Deborah managed to stand up and limp into the room, closing the door behind her. She stepped out of her breeches so stiff with blood it seemed they could practically stand by themselves. She noticed on a nearby table surgical instruments and dressings. She quickly selected a silver probe curved at one end, lint made of softened linen, a bandage and a jar of salve the surgeon had applied to her other wound.

Steeling herself, she examined her thigh. The blood was still flowing moderately from a hole about a quarter of an inch wide. Intoxicated by the wine, her nerves somewhat dulled, Deborah seized the silver probe, thrust it into the open wound in an effort to extricate the ball embedded about an inch into her thigh. Excruciating as they felt, her first two attempts failed. But on the third try, as she prayed to God for help, she twisted the ball out of resistant and fiery flesh.

The agonizing ordeal over, Deborah put salve on the bleeding wound, placed the lint over it, then the bandage. She wrung out her breeches in a washtub, hung them over a chair to dry.

Seeing a loose white hospital gown dangling on a wall nail, Deborah took it, wrapped it around her. She then lay down on a mattress of straw which she assumed was a hospital cot, wishing she could sleep for weeks.

At that moment the French surgeon walked in. He asked, "How are you?"

"Fine," she said.

She saw doubt in his perceptive, brown eyes. Quickly she reassured him, "I need sleep, I didn't have much last night," then closed her eyes and either fainted or fell asleep.

It seemed only seconds later she awoke to see the surgeon poking his finger through the hole in her wet but clean breeches hanging from the chair. Then she heard him ask, "How came this?"

She tried to think clearly, not an easy task now that the wine was wearing off and she felt searing pain from the wound. She said, "There was a nail in the horse's saddle. It scratched me."

She wanted only that he disappear and let her sleep. She had less fear of a dozen enemy musket balls than his penetrating glance, one that might uncover her deeper lie. Then suddenly the surgeon seemed to accept her version of the cause of the hole, turned away.

She stayed at the field hospital three days, sleeping most of the time. As she felt better, she thought the young surgeon's scrutiny diminished in intensity. It was almost as though he suspected she suffered a more serious wound but honored her secrecy in hiding it.

She did not want to risk further chance of discovery, should he ask her to disrobe so he could examine the "nail scratch" that had filled her breeches and boot with blood. Although her wound still hurt badly, she decided to leave at the first opportunity.

When two of the three other wounded soldiers recovered she asked to accompany them to Verplanck's, limped the several miles north. An army barge took them up the river to the fortress.

Colonel Jackson praised the volunteer scouting party for its successful retaliation—another major triumph in Deborah's army career. The party had taken nine prisoners and seven badly needed horses. No one knew how many Tories had been wounded or killed. One of their own men had been slain and six, including Deborah, wounded.

She defiantly refused to go to the hospital at the fortress, which took care of the wounded and the victims of epidemics of smallpox, diphtheria, malaria, typhus, dysentery and scurvy. Each regiment had a surgeon and his assistant, a mate appointed by the director of the hospital.

The saber slash across her forehead healed quickly, leaving only the slightest of scars. But the wound in her thigh was slow to mend. Each day the compulsory drilling would start it bleeding again. Two weeks later when she took part in a march to a place in the neutral territory called Collebarack, her leg ached so she could barely move.

Suddenly a soldier named Snow, marching beside Deborah, stumbled, fell, then lay on the ground as if in a coma. The sergeant felt Snow's forehead, concluded he had a high fever.

"He can't go on and we can't leave him," said the sergeant.

Deborah saw a mansion off in the distance. A way of protecting herself while continuing to serve in her beloved army occurred to her. Pointing to the mansion, she said to the sergeant, "Maybe they'd let Snow stay there until he feels better. I don't feel so well myself but I could look after him."

The sergeant agreed to the idea. Several of the men carried Snow to the mansion, knocked on the door. It was opened by a plump man of about fifty who smiled rather insincerely, Deborah thought. With eyes narrowing as he saw they were Continental Army soldiers, he asked, "What can I do for you?"

"Do you own this house?" asked the sergeant.

He said he did, his name was Van Tassel. The sergeant asked if he could leave two sick soldiers there for a few days while they recovered. Van Tassel agreed to take care of them.

But when the door closed behind the rest of the party, he turned to Deborah who was holding up Snow and snarled, "Follow me."

He led her through several rooms, portraits of distinguished men on the walls. Without looking back he swiftly walked up a flight of stairs. Deborah, supporting Snow, staggered after him, Snow in such pain he could hardly make it even with her help. She was distressed to see there was still another long flight to the garret.

She protested to Van Tassel, "This man is very ill. Can't you find him a bed on the second floor?"

"The attic floor is good enough for rebels," he curtly replied.

He herded them into a small, dirty garret, hot as a desert with August heat. He left without a word, not even offering a drink of water.

Deborah lay on the floor next to the agonized Snow for hours, ill and in pain from her wound, perspiring, bitten by mosquitoes. But worst of all, she was famished, not having eaten all day. She wondered if Van Tassel intended to starve them to death as the British did the patriots on prison ships. As she lay there she recalled with horror the most infamous prison ship of all, the *Jersey*, where once healthy Continental Army soldiers were reduced to skeletons in tattered shreds, feverish, starved, victims of smallpox, crawling with vermin and roaches, the air filled with the ravings of the delirious and the moans of the dying.

That evening Deborah, hearing a soft knock on the door, was filled with a sudden fright that Van Tassel was returning to kill them. Instead, she was delighted when a pretty girl in her late teens entered with a tray of bread, cheese and wine. The girl introduced herself as Van Tassel's daughter and promised to bring the sick soldiers some food each evening. Deborah thanked her, then tried to get Snow to sip the wine and swallow some of the cheese. But he turned away from the food and drink as though they were poison.

Each evening the compassionate young woman brought scraps of food, apologizing because she dared not steal more from the kitchen lest her father catch her. Deborah realized Van Tassel's house was a rendezvous for Tories whom he entertained nightly after their forays. She could hear them drinking and shouting below, reveling in the spoils they had seized that day from the homes of patriots. She passed the time in dread that one night Van Tassel and his drunken Tories would burst into the attic and kill Snow and herself. Terrified of being trapped in the tiny garret, she charged both their pieces. Then she tied a rope to a ledge outside the one small window, where she planned to make their escape if necessary.

At the end of the seventh night, Snow died. Deborah felt like crying but no tears flowed. She thought how casually one could accept the death of a stranger. She had narrowly escaped death recently, was not out of danger herself. At the thought of being alone with the dead soldier left in her care, she stopped feeling anything. It was not until three days later she was able to acknowledge her deep grief.

She sat at the garret window inhaling the air. She watched a party of Tories ride up to the house as Van Tassel walked out to greet them. She wryly observed how differently he treated the Tories than Snow and herself. She felt furious as she heard the Tories boast from the ground below that the horses they rode were stolen from "the rebels."

In horror she suddenly saw several starved cats from adjacent garrets swarm into the room, leap onto Snow's corpse and begin to eat it. She wrapped Snow's slender body in a protective blanket, shut the door against the hungry cats, sending up the temperature in the already hot room.

Without Snow to care for, Deborah knew she need stand no more of the daily torture. At daybreak, the Tories gone, she stole down the stairs to the first floor. There she was chagrined to find the front door locked. As she was returning to the garret to escape through the window, she met Van Tassel's daughter stepping out of her bedroom on the second floor.

Deborah apologized for waking her and the young woman invited her into the dining room where she poured each of them a glass of Madeira, evidently wanting to talk. She told Deborah she regretted her father's cruel treatment, saying his behavior caused her mother and her much suffering, since they were humane people who were not Tories. The girl seemed reluctant to have Deborah leave but agreed to unlock the front door. Deborah assured her that she would never forget such kindness.

In the early morning light Deborah walked softly away from the Van Tassel mansion and the corpse of the young soldier she had hoped to save. On the trail she met soldiers of her regiment heading home from a scouting mission, returned with them to West Point.

After her first comfortable night's sleep in ten days, Deborah asked permission to speak to Colonel Jackson. She entered his office, saluted, opened her mouth to speak. But before she could utter a word, he said, "Private Shurtliff, I hear reports of your courage under fire and I must commend your willingness to take on dangerous situations."

Deborah managed to squelch the burst of pride that all but enveloped her. She answered modestly, "I do my best, sir."

The colonel then asked what he could do for her. She explained Van Tassel was a Tory sympathizer who entertained loyalist troops at night after they ransacked patriot homes. She said that Private Snow lay dead because Van Tassel had refused to give him food or a bed and that she now would like to help organize a scouting party to return to the Van Tassel mansion, avenge Snow's death and return his body for a proper burial.

"Please, sir," she said, her frozen feelings thawing, "I sat with Private Snow for seven days and nights and watched him die in that stifling garret, starved like a rat by Van Tassel."

"All right, Private Shurtliff," said Colonel Jackson, "go after your revenge."

A scouting party was organized to return to the Van Tassel mansion to capture the Tories and pick up Snow's body. They set out for Verplanck's, which provided each brigade with a separate landing, in the order of its encamping. These landings, according to General Washington, were "for the purpose of removing baggage and for embarking and debarking the troops with facility." The brigadier who supervised the barge operations had been ordered "to assign four good oarsmen to each boat, and an officer who has some skill in the management, to take charge of them till further orders; they will see that scoops are provided for freeing the boats of water in case they prove leaky." Sometimes a boat sprung a leak in the middle of the river and the soldiers had to help bail out the water so they could reach the opposite shore.

Deborah's scouting party arrived late in the afternoon in the vicinity of the Van Tassel mansion. After eating supper rations of salt beef, peas and bread, they hid in the woods nearby, waiting for the Tories to show up in the evening to drink and boast of their latest brutalities against the "rebels."

As she rested against a tree Deborah thought how deeply she despised the turncoat Tories, yearned to steal away their dreams of looting rebel homes and killing rebel soldiers. Just after dark, they saw twenty Tories ride up to the mansion. The sergeant leading the scouting party whispered to her, "Let's get them."

"Wait until they're drunk," she suggested. "It will be easier."

By midnight she decided the Tories would be reveling and off guard. She silently led the scouting party onto the Van Tassel grounds. Then they burst into the house and pointed their muskets at the astounded Tories.

The sergeant barked, "You're all as good as dead if you don't give yourselves up as prisoners of war." He turned to Van Tassel, said, "If you don't stop entertaining Tories who have robbed patriot homes, we're coming back to take you as prisoner."

Van Tassel's face contorted in hate as he saw Deborah, knowing "Private Shurtliff" had led the raid in revenge for Van Tassel's treatment of the sick soldier. Deborah looked for his daughter but evidently she had retreated to her room.

Without shedding one drop of blood but causing tears to flow— some of the Tories cried in their drunkenness when captured—the scouting party took twenty Tories and nine horses found in the stables. The soldiers marched prisoners and horses back to West Point. Two of the soldiers carried Snow's body.

The next evening Colonel Jackson summoned Deborah to his quarters, handed her a bottle of Madeira as her reward and suggested she share it with the soldiers who had accompanied her.

"How about a bottle for the prisoners?" she asked.

Colonel Jackson looked astonished. "Would you give wine to men who would gladly murder us?"

"They're human, too," she said, not wishing to be like Van Tassel, who abused and starved his enemy. "Maybe we can make converts of them if we treat them well."

The colonel handed her a second bottle and Deborah took it to the prisoners. Generous, if also naive, she unloosened the hands of a Tory sergeant so he could drink. He took a long swig from the bottle. But when she tried to retie his hands, he struck her to the ground. Feeling betrayed, she slowly picked herself up. He started to hit her again but one of the patriot soldiers subdued him.

Another Tory said to the sergeant jeeringly, "That's a poor way to treat a host who offers you a drink."

The Tory sergeant turned to Deborah and said, a look of loathing on his face, "By God, you not only insult me by taking me prisoner, but you steal my girl."

Deborah was puzzled. "What do you mean?" she asked.

"Old man Van Tassel's daughter is in love with you," he answered.

Shocked, Deborah realized this might be true. Without any intent on her part, as courageous Robert Shurtliff, soldier of the Continental Army, she had won for the moment the uncertain heart of a seventeen-year-old girl.

The Tory sergeant received fifty lashes on his naked back for his attack on Deborah, then was tried with the rest of the Tories and imprisoned at Fishkill.

Slowly her painful wound was healing. After the field hospital experience she was particularly careful to protect herself from discovery. Every so often something would happen to quicken her fear. For a few days, one of her tentmates was Ebenezer Morton, Jr., from Middleborough, who had often seen her in feminine dress. But even in these close quarters he gave no more sign of recognizing her than did Colonel Ebenezer Sproat, owner of Sproat Tavern in Middleborough. Nevertheless she was thankful when Morton was reassigned to New Windsor.

She was afraid her hands might give her away as she sewed loose buttons on her waistcoat or regimental coat, mended tears in her breeches and stitched buttons on the coats of men who could not sew. She threaded a needle and sewed with more ease and grace than the men. Still no one commented on her obvious skills.

General Washington had instructed the officers to pay the most minute attention to the soldier's "method of priming and loading, as well as leveling and taking aim" when it came to military training, which he thought essential. But he also thought important the military appearance of the men. He was always sending orders that directed the men to look neat, keep their clothing in the best possible repair. He criticized "ill-fitting uniforms" and the lack of hats and shoes that often occurred, since they, particularly the black leather shoes, were difficult to obtain in the quantity needed. One order from the general read: "It is now considered that not only the comfort and convenience, but even the reputation of the corps depend essentially upon keeping every article belonging to the soldier in the most perfect state, both for service and appearance."

This drew grumbles from the men, although the companies then felt forced to hire their own washerwoman. Deborah insisted on washing her uniform in a barrel at night, wearing overalls and a waistcoat if she also needed to wash a shirt.

The soldiers kept their regimental coats in fairly good condition by turning them inside out at times, or wearing only shirt and waistcoat in warm weather, and substituting woolen waistcoats to protect themselves in the cold. If the officer of the day was not strict, the men could leave off their regimental coats as they drilled and even during marches. But coats were required on special occasions such as inspections, reviews and grand parades.

Throughout the army, a soldier's hair was cut and tied in the familiar queue. General Washington sent word to the officers that "to wear the hair cut or tied in the same manner throughout a whole corps would still be a very considerable improvement; where it cannot be done in a regiment similarity in a company would add much to the beauty of it."

An order from the general on August 12 stipulated that two hundred pounds of flour and a half pound of tallow per one hundred men be granted for hair dressing. The men might not be equal in economic status, in literacy or the social graces but when it came to the style of their hair, all were the same.

For the first time in the life of Deborah Sampson, she shared full equality with a man, even unto the way her hair was styled.

REMEMBRANCE
OF LIFE PAST

One day Deborah heard her real name spoken and was struck rigid with shock. A sergeant was telling a private that a strange man was wandering through the barracks looking for a woman named Deborah Sampson. He said she might have joined the army dressed as a male. The sergeant and the private laughed at the idea as though it were the most ludicrous in the world.

Deborah thought the man searching for her had to be the one her mother wanted her to marry. She was curious to find out if this were true. Feeling secure enough in her assumed sexual identity to risk exposure, she started for the barracks. On the way, she saw a tall, familiar figure walking toward her.

She lowered her eyes to the ground as they passed. She felt fairly safe. He could not possibly believe the pale, well-groomed, soft-voiced Deborah Sampson of Middleborough was this sun-burnt, powder-burnt West Point private with the weather-beaten complexion, complete with calloused, rough hands and broken nails.

For a moment her eyes filled with tears. Not for the love of this man, for she had never deceived herself she loved him, but because he cared enough to search for her—and because the sight of him revived memories, especially of her mother who had urged her so persistently to marry him.

Deborah knew she had been cruel in not telling her mother the reason for her mysterious flight. This was the first time in Deborah's life she had not kept in touch with her mother, who had never lived more than fifteen miles away.

Not hearing a word from her daughter in months, her mother must have imagined Deborah's body decaying in some dark woods outside Middleborough. She probably believed Deborah had chosen to kill herself rather than marry a man she did not love—a man she thought foolish and irresponsible despite the fact his father was a respectable merchant.

She had met this man in her mother's home in Plymouth. Her mother and the man's father obviously arranged what they hoped would be a loving match. The night Deborah had decided she would never marry him, he rode over on his horse from Plymouth, liquor already on his breath. They went to Sproat Tavern where she drank her usual glass of rum and he had two flips. Fully intoxicated, he rambled wildly about how happy they would be raising a large family. He never once asked how she felt about such a future, or if she accepted his proposal of marriage.

She had turned her face away, thought, *Never.* She could not bring herself to marry a man who drank heavily like her father.

Jonathan Sampson had started to drink after his father died in 1757, three years before Deborah was born. His father, who owned hundreds of acres in Plympton, had left no will for his six daughters and one son, born late in his mother's life.

As the only son, Deborah's father had expected from an early age to be heir to the largest part of the acreage. But, according to him, a dishonest brother-in-law had led to his being "robbed" of his share. In a pique, he sold his inheritance to one of his sisters and her husband, Joseph Perry. After that he spent his afternoons and evenings at the tavern. Deborah's mother, a competent woman standing in the shoes of an absent man, ran the farm with the help of her older sons.

Deborah's grandfather, Jonathan Sampson, Sr., had cleared wilderness to build the house in which she was born. It had a large, square chimney, a low-pitched roof and a spring well in the front. There were two small bedrooms, one at each end. The kitchen had a large fireplace, as did the eastern bedroom. The wood, inside and out, was dark unpainted pine. All the rooms had corner posts and ceiling beams. There were twenty-four panes in the windows. (She once counted them.)

Deborah was born in one of the back bedrooms during wintry weather, on December 17, 1760, in Plympton, originally called Winnetuxet by the Indians. As Plymouth's population grew, the early settlers moved to the outlying countryside where they built cottages and cultivated the land. They were required to travel to Plymouth for Sunday church services until the general court finally permitted them to build their own churches.

Deborah's great-grandfather, Isaac Sampson, was one of the first settlers of Plympton. The family was proud of town records showing Plympton inhabitants had voted in 1720 "to give Isaac Sampson twenty-five shillings for sweeping the Meetinghouse and taking care of open and shut doors and shutting the casements if they happen to be left open."

Isaac's father, Abraham Sampson, had arrived in Plymouth in August 1629 from Leyden, Holland, nine years after his brother Henry had sailed over on the *Mayflower*. Abraham settled in Duxbury with his brother, married Lydia Standish and had four sons, Samuel, George, Abraham and Isaac.

The Sampson coat of arms, of which Deborah's father had a copy, was a cross between two escallops, a very ancient insignia, with the motto, "Disgrace is worse than death." The cross, with flowers at the four ends, denoted that the first bearer of the arms took part in the early religious wars. The escallops or scallop shells was a very old and honorable emblem, indicating a pilgrimage which in all likelihood was the Crusades.

Her father's side thus boasted distinguished ancestors. Through him, Deborah was descended from the red-haired Miles Standish and John Alden, two other men who came over on the *Mayflower*. Isaac's wife Lydia was the granddaughter of Sir Miles, the military leader of the pilgrims. Lydia's mother was Sarah Alden, daughter of John and Priscilla Alden. Deborah felt delighted to think that the daughter of Priscilla and John Alden married the son of Miles Standish and his wife, Barbara. Even if Miles Standish never won the heart of Priscilla, lost to John Alden when she said, "Why don't you speak for yourself, John?", his son had married her daughter, thus achieving true poetic justice.

Deborah's grandfather, Jonathan Sampson, Sr., the son of Isaac and Lydia Sampson, was born February 9, 1690. He married Joanna Lucas on September 28, 1721, they had six daughters and one son, Jonathan Sampson Jr., Deborah's father, born in Plympton on April 3, 1729. He was twenty-two years old when he married Deborah Bradford on November 1, 1751.

Deborah Bradford's ancestors were equally illustrious. Her great-grandfather was William Bradford, who also came over on the *Mayflower*. He was the second governor of Plymouth Colony, following John Carver and Massachusetts' foremost citizen for thirty-seven years. He spoke not only French and Dutch but Latin, Greek and Hebrew. He was known for his unselfish public spirit, wisdom and sense of justice. At his death on May 9, 1657, he was described as "a common blessing and father to all the colonies." He was the first historian of the Plymouth Colony.

Deborah read with pride her great-great-grandfather's journal in which he wrote, in enumerating the "sundrie weightie and solid reasons" for the pilgrims leaving England, that they did not emigrate for "newfangledness or other such like giddie humor" but found "the hardnes of the place and countrie to be such as few in comparison would continew with them. For many that came to them and many more that desired to be with them could not endure that great labor and hard fare with other inconveniences which they underwent and were contented with."

Governor Bradford's son, Joseph, born in 1630 to the governor's second wife, Alice Carpenter Southworth, married Jael Hobart, daughter of the Reverend Peter Hobart, first minister of Hingham, in 1664. They lived in Kingston, then part of Plymouth and had a son, Elisha.

Elisha was Deborah's grandfather. His second wife, whom he married September 7, 1719, after the death of his first wife, Hannah Cole, possessed the romantic name of Bathsheba Le Broche. Bathsheba, Deborah's grandmother, was to have an inordinate influence on her life and subsequent choice of career. She was a young French woman of beauty and elegance, whose father had brought her to the colonies from Paris. She and Elisha lived in Scituate and had fifteen children, of whom Deborah's mother was the ninth. Elisha, who had a literary turn of mind, was a rich man until a ship carrying a valuable cargo of iron ore, for which he was underwriter, sank in mid-ocean. He died shortly after, perhaps from a broken spirit.

Deborah's grandmother, the spirited Bathsheba, was very close to her daughter Deborah, often visited her grandchildren in Plympton. She spoiled young Deborah outrageously, according to Deborah's mother, as Deborah, with her bright mind and warm, affectionate nature, became Bathsheba's favorite. Deborah remembered her grandmother telling her many times in her French accent the inspiring story of the heroine of France, Joan of Arc, the Maid of Orleans who in a pair of breeches led the French army to victory over the British. She was burned at the stake for her bravery because she insisted she was responsible only to God and not to the hypocritical rulers of the church.

Deborah's grandmother also told her she had named Deborah's mother after the woman warrior of biblical history, a lovely and witty woman described in the Book of Judges, who sat under a palm tree in the country of Ephraim. When the people came to Deborah for a judgment on the enemy, the King of Canaan, she sent for Barak, the general of the King of Canaan's army. Barak said he would not fight unless Deborah went with him. She pointed out that if she did, a woman would get credit for the victory. He said he did not care. So, with Deborah at his side, Barak defeated the soldiers of Sisera with their nine hundred chariots of iron, killing them all except the general, who fled.

These were the two stories of her childhood that made the deepest impression on Deborah—the heroism of the Maid of Orleans and the biblical woman after whom Deborah was named. Both fought in a war alongside men, not afraid to risk their lives to save their country.

These two women became Deborah's ideals, the heroines Grandmother Bathsheba admired most. Deborah adored her grandmother, wished to be loved by her. What better way to become number one in her grandmother's esteem than to emulate her heroines? People frequently become what their given names destined them to be. Named for the biblical Deborah, little Deborah was preordained at birth to become a woman warrior.

When she was five Deborah mourned two crippling losses. First her adored grandmother died but the ideals she had instilled in little Deborah became a deep part of her as she kept alive her cherished grandmother within her. Then, just after her grandmother's death an even greater loss struck the heart of the bereaved little girl. Deborah's father announced he was sailing for England to seek his fortune, saying there was nothing left for him in the wilderness of America.

Deborah remembered well the day he left. She climbed on a chair by the window and pressed her face against the panes. She watched her father's husky figure slowly walk away from their home, carrying a satchel filled with his clothes. Her eyes followed him down the dirt path to the road, then as he turned left toward the sea that would carry him off. She kept him in sight as long as she could until he vanished. She wondered if she would ever see him again.

Deborah was to remember that day forever. She sensed the ghastly hollow in the center of her being that her father's desertion created. He had deserted not only Deborah but his wife, pregnant with her eighth and last child. A little girl, Sylvia, was born five months later. Because Deborah was named after her mother she undoubtedly felt more special than Sylvia, as though her mother had loved only her enough to bestow her own name.

Her mother's first child was Robert Shurtliff Sampson, born in 1752 a year after her parents married. He died when he was eight. It is questionable whether a mother ever completely recovers from the death of a child. In all likelihood Mrs. Sampson continued to mourn Robert all her life. A mother in mourning is often emotionally unavailable to her other children. Deborah, a sensitive child who loved her mother, understood her grief and wanted in some way to alleviate it.

As war raged she may have felt she had to replace her dead brother in order to possess her mother's love. When she chose his name as she joined the army, a part of her was saying, "See, Mother, Robert lives! I've given him back to you. Come out of your shell and be happy. Then you will be there for me, too."

The second child, Jonathan, was born in 1753, then Elisha in 1755, Hannah, the first girl, in 1756, Ephraim in 1759, Deborah in 1760 and Nehemiah in 1764. The three older boys no doubt slept in one bedroom, Hannah, Nehemiah and Deborah in another and her mother and the baby Sylvia in the third.

Their food was simple but nourishing, with an occasional banquet of venison or beef. The meals did not change after her father's departure as her mother and older sons ran the farm. For Sunday breakfast Mrs. Sampson stirred corn batter in a large iron pan and made griddle cakes, which the family drowned with molasses.

Mrs. Sampson taught Deborah to wash her face and hands twice a day, brush her teeth with a hickory toothbrush every morning. These habits stood Deborah in good stead in the army. Her mother also taught her the alphabet and simple words when she first started to speak.

One day Mrs. Sampson was informed that the stagecoach had left a letter addressed to her at the general store. She walked half a mile for the letter. When she returned, her eyes were red from tears. She told the children their father and all hands had been lost at sea in a furious storm that wrecked his ship off England. The letter was from the owner of the vessel.

The thought of never seeing her father again devastated Deborah, she felt crushed. She had memories of his holding her as she inhaled the fragrance of tobacco and sometimes rum on his breath.

He was the protector of the home, the big strong father who kept them safe. How would they manage without him?

She still had the memory of watching him take a musket and shoot the crows and blackbirds that ate the corn. This taught her it was proper to kill a hated enemy who threatened her survival. The town had voted that every house owner had to kill either two crows or six blackbirds, or six of any other bird that destroyed corn, such as the jaybird or brown woodpecker or squirrels and bring in their heads to the selectmen. Those who "refused" or "neglected" this duty were ordered to pay two shillings as a fine.

Deborah would forever love her father with all the fire in her five-year-old heart. She had his hazel-blue eyes, thick blond hair and was tall, in his image. She grew up to be somewhat like him, possessing the same spirit of adventure. She, too, she often thought, would someday leave home on an important mission.

At first Deborah's mother tried to keep her family together. But prices were steep and she could not afford to feed the children. Butter was six cents a pound, meat twelve, and a cod, four. She was forced to ask relatives to help out. They offered to take her five oldest children into their homes. In this way the children escaped having their names read at the town meeting and taken into the houses of strangers as objects of charity or public charges. Her mother kept the baby and Nehemiah, the second youngest child, with her as she moved in with her brother Nehemiah, who lived in Plymouth.

Thus when Deborah was five-and-a-half years old, it was decided she would live with her mother's cousin, Ruth Fuller, a woman who had never married. She resided in Middleborough, four miles to the southwest of Plympton. Deborah was taken there by her mother in a farmer's cart with her few possessions—a calico dress for summer, a linsey-woolsey for winter, a petticoat, white knit socks, a heavy coat, woolen hat and mittens.

As her home in Plympton disappeared from sight, Deborah must have felt she had no one left in the world who cared about her. She had lost her idolized father, her beloved grandmother and now her mother, brothers and sisters. Even if she had lived next door, she would have felt abandoned, thrown out of her own home, her own room. She could not help a pang of jealousy at the thought that Nehemiah and the baby Sylvia were permitted to stay with their mother. Neither a baby nor a small boy, Deborah thought of herself ever after, she would tell Mann, as "born unfortunate, my sun clouded."

But Cousin Fuller proved a kind woman and living with her did not seem particularly traumatic for Deborah. She gave Deborah a room of her own, sewed her pretty new dresses, provided nourishing food and bought fancy sweetmeats from the peddler who stopped by occasionally. Cousin Fuller also taught Deborah, hungry to learn and spell new words, some of the more complicated ones, read to her from the Bible. She repaid the kindness by helping around the house, washing dishes, brushing up the ashes in the fireplace with the sedge broom, making the beds.

For three years Deborah lived with her aunt until Cousin Fuller suddenly fell seriously ill and within a few days died in her home. Fortunately, the Reverend Sylvanus Conant, minister of the First Congregational Church of Middleborough, had taken an interest in the eight-year-old friendly child. When Deborah's mother arrived from Plymouth, he suggested Deborah live at the home of the widow of the Reverend Peter Thacher, his predessessor at the church. Mrs. Thacher was eighty years old and ailing but there was a servant at her house so Deborah would be required to do only some of the smaller tasks. It did not seem to occur to Deborah's mother or the Reverend Conant that an eighty-year-old woman was not a very suitable companion for an eight-year-old girl.

Deborah liked the Reverend Conant, who occasionally brought

her books to read and seemed to care about what happened to her. He arranged for her to ride at times to Plymouth with Benjamin Thomas in his farmer's cart so she could visit her mother. She sat beside Mr. Thomas as he held the reins, asked questions about the sky at night: Did anyone live on the planets and stars? How far away were they? He was a friendly man who seemed to enjoy her company. He told her he had seven sons and he and his wife were expecting another child they hoped would be a girl.

At Mrs. Thacher's house Deborah was now asked to do the heavy work, carrying water from the well, washing the clothes, scouring the pots, emptying the slops. She never complained to her mother but after Deborah had lived at Mrs. Thacher's for two years, her mother decided, upon visiting her daughter and noticing the heavy duties required of her, that they were too taxing for her ten-year-old child.

Mrs. Sampson again consulted Reverend Conant. He told her that Benjamin Thomas and his wife, now the parents of eight sons, who lived on a vast farm, were looking for a helper. Deborah's mother decided to place her in the Thomas home as an indentured servant until she was eighteen.

Once again Deborah made a packet of her few belongings. Mr. Thomas called for her in his farmer's cart. He drove her to his home, a large house of white oak in a sheltered spot two miles east of Middleborough Four Corners, so-called because it was located at the crossroads of two main highways, one running east and west, the other, north and south.

Deborah was given a room in the loft over the kitchen. From her one window she could see trees framing the cow pasture. She had a chest for her clothes, her own candle and—what must have delighted her the most—a wooden desk Mr. Thomas built in honor of her arrival. On it she kept birch paper, a goose quill and homemade ink. Like Benjamin Franklin, she wrote daily of her good deeds on one side of a page, her bad deeds on the other, she later told Mann. No doubt the good side was lengthier than the bad.

She enjoyed the quiet hours of night as she snuggled in bed, the room warm from the kitchen fireplace beneath. She listened to the creaking of the house timbers as they settled, the occasional rush of the wind, the soft pelt of snow against the panes in winter.

At first Deborah was frightened at the thought of living with eight boys. But following their mother and father's example, the boys treated her courteously. They became so friendly she soon felt as though she were their sister rather than "bound out." During the eight years she stayed with the Thomases, two more sons were born. Mr. and Mrs. Thomas never achieved their wish for a girl, they had to accept Deborah as substitute.

In spite of the endless work of cooking, making clothes for, and cleaning up after her husband and sons, Mrs. Thomas was a cheerful, generous woman. She taught Deborah the fine points of cooking, baking bread, grinding dried herbs with mortar and pestle. She also taught her how to make rag rugs, sew samplers, spin and weave lawn and muslin from the flax they grew in the fields, as well as fustian and serge from the soft mounds of wool Mr. Thomas and his sons sheared from their own sheep.

It was at the Thomases' home Deborah learned the arts of weaving and spinning, later giving her the reputation of "the most skillful spinner in town." She feared a large growth under her nail from the spinning of yarn would not disappear. It caused her to hold her quill awkwardly when she wrote. She later feared this painful, clumsy positioning of her finger might give her away on her first attempt to join the army. Eventually she wrote once again in normal fashion as the growth vanished.

Mrs. Thomas never ordered Deborah to do things like carry the ashes to the pit behind the barn or scrub a peck of potatoes from the root cellar. Instead, she gently requested. She always seemed concerned about Deborah's needs, treating the lone girl in the house with care and respect.

She described to Deborah in a quiet, unalarming way the monthly flow of blood all women went through, explaining this was necessary in order to have babies. Deborah was grateful for the warning, otherwise when she first became aware of her period she might have thought she was bleeding to death, punished by God for some awful sin. Like stealing a second portion of the plum pudding or taking the name of the Lord in vain when she cut her finger on the scythe.

Mrs. Thomas made sure Deborah had new shoes when the cobbler came to fit the family. She bought Deborah brightly colored kerchiefs for her dresses, linen aprons, combs and a looking glass to see herself as she ran a comb through her blond curls.

Deborah helped care for the two babies when they were born, bathing them, dressing them, rocking them in their cradles, washing their diapers and hanging them by the fire. As the little boys grew older she read to them from *The Shorter Catechism of the Assembly of the Divines*, told them Bible stories.

While Mrs. Thomas was a gentle, generous woman, Deborah's character also contributed to the good fit in the household. She was a cheerful, uncomplaining helper to the whole family. Her warm care of the two babies in particular greatly eased the hardships of the overburdened mother of ten sons and improved the quality of life for the rest of the family.

Because the farm was large, Deborah helped feed the cows, pigs and chickens, tend the sheep, rake hay. She took pride in being able to handle farm implements as skillfully as the boys. She also learned to fashion a basket, build a milking stool, carve a weather-cock with a jackknife.

Although she did not particularly relish the care and feeding of animals, Deborah felt a natural love of the vegetable and herb gardens, planting dill, fennel and caraway. The latter was used as "meeting seeds," on which the children were permitted to munch during Sunday church services. Deborah planted corn under the guidance of Mr. Thomas, who said the Indians had warned the pilgrims not to plant one kernel "until the buds on the oak trees were the size of a mouse's ear." She gathered apples in the fall for eating, cooking or drying, helped fry or cut them up for apple pies.

Deborah enjoyed the kitchen fragrances, the bread baking in the oven, the tasty duck roasting, the puddings steaming. She spent many happy moments in the low-ceilinged Thomas kitchen with its great open hearth, Dutch oven, long red oak table with benches along its sides. Pewter mugs and crockery decorated the wall shelves, pans, iron and copper kettles hung over the fireplace.

To help Mrs. Thomas, Deborah made patchwork quilts, spun and sewed suits for Mr. Thomas and the boys, stuffed feather beds, including one for herself. If there were time she was allowed to attend school but usually asked the older boys to catch her up on lessons. She would thoughtfully study their schoolbooks, use quill and ink to copy long words and sentences.

She read late at night by the brass whale-oil lamp, taking out of the Thomas library the plays of Shakespeare, the works of Swift, Dryden, Voltaire and John Locke. She felt particularly inspired by Locke's belief it was the right of man to overthrow a government that took his money or property without consent. Locke's philosophy was germane in the formation of her conviction of the right of the colonists to defeat the British tyrants—it proved instrumental in the subsequent choice that led her to join the army. She still carried an emotional torch for her father and despised the British because he had supposedly drowned as he left England, in addition to their wish to possess the colonies.

Deborah wrote in her diary thoughts about the state of the world. Mr. Thomas said one day, commenting on her bookish propensity, "Deborah, you are always either buried in some book or scrabbling over paper." He was impressed with her scholarship, intelligence and the surprising degree to which this barely schooled young woman was able to educate herself.

Mr. Thomas, a religious man who became a member of the Massachusetts state legislature, like most men of those days, thought it a waste of time for a young woman to be seen with book in hand—an unpardonable neglect in the making of yarn or the baking of bread. Deborah believed, however, that a knowledge of letters was more necessary to her than a table of dainties—that she needed mental food, like her grandfather Elisha and her grandmother and mother gave her. She thought it a fatal error of many parents that they began the education of their daughter "with a painted doll" and ended it with "a set of China tea dishes."

Some evenings Deborah and the boys would cluster around the hearth drinking hot cider, whittling cheese ladders, door latches, shoe pegs, butter paddles, hog and goose yokes, or wooden soldiers for the youngest sons. She joined the boys in the outdoor games of summer, often outrunning them. Mr. Thomas called her fleet as a gazelle.

She grew very tall, what with all the exercise and ample food, taller than the oldest Thomas boys. She asked Mr. Thomas to show her how to handle a musket and after she learned, the boys took her with them when they hunted wild turkey, partridge, deer and rabbit. They ate the turkey with rhubarb sauce, the rabbits, if not too full of buckshot, went into a stew. In time Deborah learned to shoot as accurately as the boys.

One day her mother and Sylvia, now eleven, came to visit her. Deborah and Sylvia, romping in the fields, saw a hawk circling in the sky. Deborah ran for her musket, loaded it and taking aim, fired at the hawk. Much to her delight, it fell.

Horrified, Sylvia said, "Deborah, how can you be so cruel?"

Deborah laughed. "The hawk would eat our chickens if I didn't kill it," she explained. Then she added, "Sylvia, you have to possess a courage bigger than a mustard seed if you want to live on a farm." Deborah's courage—"bigger than a mustard seed"— would some day make her an army heroine.

She learned about flowers, shrubs and trees. The white oak was the traveler's compass, the south side of the bark rough to the touch, the north, smooth. She ran barefoot in summer enjoying the feel of warm earth under her toes and soles. She found a hideout in the woods, a nook behind a large spruce fenced with rocks, but there was not much time for retreat to it. She did not think a more pleasant place could be found, though she would have preferred living the last eight years with her mother, brothers, and sisters.

Deborah had lived with the Thomas family four years when something happened that forever changed her world and the world of the colonies. The large bell in the tower of the First Presbyterian Church, heard for miles, pealed whenever there was important news. The townspeople would rush to the meeting hall to learn what exciting event had occurred.

The bell pealed on December 16, 1773, the night before Deborah's fourteenth birthday. At the meeting hall it was announced that Boston patriots—Paul Revere and John Hancock among them—disguised as Indians dumped tea belonging to the East India Company into the harbor, in protest of British taxes.

The bell pealed again in March 1774, with the news that, in

retaliation, England declared the port of Boston closed to all trading. In support of the patriots Middleborough sent eighty bushels of grain to Boston, as did other towns.

After that there was talk of little but the impending war everyone seemed to accept as inevitable. The bell rang out on April 18, 1775, announcing Paul Revere's ride to Lexington and Concord. Husbands and sons left their work in the fields, raced northwest to the scene of action. Some women and children fled to swamps and caverns for safety, believing they would be attacked by the British. Mrs. Thomas and Deborah continued the household chores.

Deborah stood on a hill near the farm, heard the British guns at Bunker Hill, saw smoke stream into the sky from houses the redcoats plundered and burned. She sent money to the poor who lost their homes, the proceeds from cloth she wove from part of the flax field Mr. Thomas assigned as her own.

Each farmer's cottage as well as the mansions of the rich became small factories of hand power, furnishing food and clothing for the army. Mr. Thomas had wool and flax in abundance and Deborah would sit winter evenings spinning by a blazing fire, listening to the hum of the wheel or the twang of the loom as Mr. Thomas read an account from the *Boston Gazette* describing the latest British atrocity.

The townspeople felt excited when they learned bog iron had been discovered in Masspoag Pond in Sharon, eighteen miles northwest. The iron would be used to make the first cannon fired at the British in Boston. This special iron of hematite was found in dark nodules in lakes and bogs, thus the name "bog iron." It had been fished up, along with sand and weeds, from Masspoag Pond, by men using tongs. A day's work filled a rowboat, supplying enough iron for a tenth of a cannon. Edmund Quincy, Jr. had found the iron ore in the pond and Colonel Richard Gridley of Boston supervised the making of the cannon. This was a very important event, as King George III had forbidden the colonies to manufacture iron, causing the Americans to be unprepared for war.

In Middleborough, Captain William Shaw began training his company of soldiers, called minutemen because they had to be ready at a minute's notice. Deborah watched them train on the lower green. Her own brothers were drilling in Plymouth. The older Thomas boys had joined the minutemen, the younger played soldiers behind the barn using sticks for guns. Mrs. Thomas and Deborah spun and wove ceaselessly, making cloth for uniforms or knit socks. Deborah could spin six skeins of wool a day, considered better than average.

Three companies of minutemen marched from Middleborough to Marshfield, near Plymouth, to suppress Tories to whom British general Thomas Gage had sent arms. When the Middleborough men returned victorious after two days, the townspeople stood at the side of the road to cheer, tears of joy in their eyes.

Mr. Thomas was chosen deacon of the First Congregational Church in 1776 and after that everyone called him Deacon Thomas. He came home from a town meeting on May 20, 1776, with the news that Middleborough, along with the other townships, had voted for America's independence from England if the Continental Congress decided to declare it.

The wild ringing of the church bells brought the family in from the fields on July 4. Deacon Thomas hitched up the cart and took them all into town to celebrate the Declaration of Independence, where emerged a spontaneous parade to the playing of fifes and drums. By now Middleborough had eight military companies who marched in special drill. They had no uniforms but they did possess muskets, musket balls and powder horns.

Congress unanimously appointed George Washington, who had fought bravely in the French and Indian Wars, as the commander in chief of the Continental Army. Deborah wistfully watched men and boys step forward to sign their names to the *Articles of Enlistment* and receive the bounty money in engraved, crisp new Continental bills. The Reverend Conant was one of the first to leave Middleborough, signing up as chaplain. Two years later, Deborah would hear he had died of smallpox. She felt bereft; this man had been considerate and kind to her when she desperately needed someone who cared after she was, in a sense, cast out of her home at five-and-a-half years old.

Over the years she visited her mother, sometimes begging rides to Plymouth on farmers' carts, for she did not have the money for stagecoach fares. At times her mother would visit her, making sure she was as happy as she could be under the sad circumstances.

Each time one of the Thomas boys said goodbye she felt saddened for they had become like her brothers—even closer, for she seldom had seen her brothers since she was five-and-a-half, whereas she had spent every day since the age of ten with the Thomases.

Deborah also yearned to enlist but knew this was a hopeless desire because she was female. Instead, all she could do was read about the war or listen to what the older folks had learned. She committed to memory some of the inspiring words of Thomas Paine from his pamphlet *Common Sense*, which she thought the literary "shot heard 'round the world," with its attack on King George III: "Of more worth is one honest man to society, and in the sight of God, than all the crowned ruffians that ever lived."

What a heroic fight, she thought, thirteen colonies scattered along more than a thousand miles of seacoast, vulnerable at every port, unprepared for war, daring to defy one of the oldest and strongest monarchies of the world. The colonies lacked a general government, they had no power to impose taxes, they had practically no navy or army. In the early days of the fighting they suffered one defeat after another, making tragic errors in military strategy.

Like every patriot, Deborah felt each victory a joyous personal triumph, each defeat a disaster. When General Washington had to retreat from New York and two thousand Continental Army troops fell into British hands, she lived with the fear her brothers or the Thomas boys were among the prisoners. She had read with deep horror of the British atrocities when General Sir William Howe and his redcoats murdered patriot soldiers captured in the Battle of Long Island on August 27, 1776. It was reported they hacked a general to pieces with cutlasses, thrust bayonets through a captain and hung privates five at a time from the limb of a white oak tree.

When Deborah's indenture to the Thomas family ended at the age of eighteen, Deacon Thomas asked what she would like to do. She said she wanted to teach school. He helped her get a job teaching boys and girls during the six-month summer session at the school in the center of town. Public education began in the Massachusetts Bay Colony in 1635, setting the pattern for the rest of the colonies.

No schoolmasters were left in Middleborough, as all the men, including Deacon Thomas, went out on alarms to help the Rhode Islanders fight off the British fleet at Newport. Deborah helped the deacon clean his musket and mold the lead balls.

She began teaching in May 1779, paid by her twenty pupils with Continental currency as well as vegetables, fruit and cloth. She taught the girls to sew and knit, the boys penmanship. Her textbooks were a Bible, a few psalters, a spelling book, copies of *The New England Primer* and her copy of *Gulliver's Travels* from which she read to the class. She was pleased when one lad she thought very intelligent brought to school a fugitive copy of Fisher's *Young Man's Best Companion*. She felt parents withheld from primary schools books that enlarged a child's capacity for wisdom and knowledge.

In the summer she lived with the Thomases, during the winter stayed in various homes in Middleborough where she could make her keep and meals by spinning and weaving cloth. She would board at one house for several weeks, and when the family's needs for cloth were met, she would move on to another. She went from the Mortons to the Clarks to the Sproat family at Sproat Tavern, where a signboard hanging outside announced "Entertainment for All Sons of Liberty," for those who stayed overnight or dropped in to eat and drink.

Deborah would sit at the spinning wheel barely speaking, without stopping to rest, sometimes from sunrise to sunset, like her ancestor Governor Bradford, who had worked as a weaver of serge and fustian in Holland. She also carved pie crimpers out of wood, sold them for fifty cents apiece.

The Revolution instilled an electric spirit throughout the colonies yet there was also underlying grimness as almost all the farmers' sons went off to war. The statesmen, lawyers and men of commerce had started the Revolution with their eloquent words but it was the farmers who bore arms and whose blood was shed.

Deacon Thomas had brought Deborah up to be very religious. Over the years she had faithfully attended Sunday worship in the imposing First Congregationalist Church on the upper green at the east end of town. She sat through hour after hour of prayers and sermons every Sunday of her life. In the winter at church she kept her mittens on, put her feet against the small iron foot warmer filled with coals.

She had never felt committed to any one religious denomination, believing only in the principles of Christianity. She deplored the fanaticism of religion as it existed in what she thought of as "the witch-and-wizard times" of Cotton Mather. She was not alone in her feeling for in 1763 Mather's Boston home had been bombed.

Deborah early fulfilled one duty to her mother, to learn like a parrot the literal answer to the question "What is the chief end of man?" She glorified God in her own way, as she later told Herman Mann. She did not believe Him entrenched in state far above the sky but as riding in the whirlwind, whispering in the zephyrs, blazing in the midst of lightning and thunder. She did not see why the field or cottage should not be a place of private worship in addition to the more public church. What she called a "seventh-day only religion, put under the carpet on weekdays, turned loose on Sundays, trimmed and starched like a new doll," seemed farcical.

After the death of the Reverend Conant a series of revival meetings attracted her to the Third Baptist Church. The Reverend Asa Hunt was the minister and her distant relative, Noah Alden of Bellingham, sometimes preached there in an exchange of pulpits.

Deborah made her first real move of independence on November 12, 1780 when she decided to renounce the religion of her Puritan ancestors and join the Baptist Church. She did not believe a town should be forced to pay taxes as Middleborough did to any one church but that each man or woman should be allowed to decide where, if and when they wished to worship.

In addition to thinking for herself, a biological factor no doubt operated within Deborah at the age of twenty. She always had been a "good girl," and the act of finally defying both Deacon Thomas and her mother was a healthy if somewhat belated adolescent rebellion. Her private revolution gave her the courage for even greater future rebelliousness. Such successful defiance was instrumental in her emotional development as she became her own person, even at the risk of losing the love of those dearest to her. Both Deacon Thomas and her mother were upset but did nothing drastic to interfere with her decision.

As Deborah was weaving at the Sproat Tavern in the winter of
1780, Deacon Thomas arrived there in anguish one day to tell her
two of his sons had been killed in Virginia, fighting with troops
commanded by the Marquis de Lafayette. She felt grief-stricken
and angry at the loss of these two young men she loved as brothers.
She wished once again she could be allowed to fight as a man, this
time to avenge their deaths. She could handle a musket as well as a
man, work as hard as a man in the fields, skin a deer or rabbit, ride
a horse, run a dairy—there was nothing a man could do in the
open that she could not do. Why should she not be allowed to fight
on the battlefields beside a man?

Deborah in a sense, was born to war. From as far back as she
could remember there had been talk of conflict. She had listened to
many a conversation between her mother and grandmother about
how war had affected the Bradfords. Governor Bradford's son,
William, commander of the Plymouth forces in King Phillip's
War, was hit at the Narragansett Fort fight by a musket ball,
which he carried the rest of his life. William's grandson, Joshua,
and his wife Hannah had been killed by Indians in Maine. Deborah's uncle, Zebulon Waters, was one of the soldiers who removed
French colonists known as Acadians from Nova Scotia in 1757.
(Many of the neutral French settled in safety in Massachusetts,
including Plympton, in the same year.)

A few women had actually fought on the battlefields of the
Revolution. In 1776 at Fort Washington, New York, Margaret
Corbin filled the post of her husband, killed by her side, until she
was so badly wounded she was disabled for life. At the Battle of
Monmouth in Jersey, Mary "Molly" Pitcher Hays carried water to
exhausted soldiers on a hot June day in 1778 until her husband was
injured, whereupon she seized his gun and fought as fiercely as any
man.

The idea occurred to Deborah that a woman might join the
Continental Army and fight side by side with the men not if she

wore skirts but if she could get away with dressing like a man.
What if no one knew she was a woman?

She was tall like a man, she had the strength and energy of a
man. All she needed was a suit and shoes like she wore at the farm
when she was in the fields.

The idea kept haunting her as she worked at the spinning wheel
and loom during the winter of 1782—a most important winter in
her life. The war was in its sixth year. She was living at the home of
Mr. and Mrs. Benjamin Leonard whose son Samuel had just gone
to war. Mrs. Leonard had turned her son's quarters into the loom
room.

There was a large chest in the corner of the room and one day
Deborah summoned the courage to open it. It contained a suit of
Samuel's, along with shirts, boots, socks and a cap. Deborah was
about Samuel's size and thought she would try the outfit on. If it fit
she would find out if she could masquerade as a man. If nobody
recognized her, she would seek the local recruiting office.

One afternoon when the Leonards had left the house Deborah
called in Jenny, the daughter of a black slave, who worked in the
Leonard home. She asked Jenny for help in changing clothes,
trusted Jenny with her secret. At first Jenny seemed shocked at
Deborah's plan but helped her dress, tied her hair back in the
masculine queue as Deborah planned for what turned out to be a
rehearsal for her final daring act.

Sproat Tavern had posted a sign announcing a fortune teller was
visiting and would foretell the future for a few pennies. Deborah
had decided to visit him, see if she could pass as a man and also
receive some word of her future.

She walked the half mile to the tavern, sought out the fortune
teller. He asked the date of her birth. When she told him December 17, he said she was born under the sign of Sagittarius, which
meant she had a zest for travel and adventure. She admitted she was

planning a trip but was not sure she had the strength to carry through on her journey.

He told her she seemed a very intelligent young gentleman and should not be afraid to act on "his" wishes. He encouraged her not to delay the trip but set off immediately.

That was all Deborah wanted to know. After he called her "a young gentleman," she made up her mind. She bid him goodbye, fled without waiting to hear further news of her future.

The fortune teller had given her courage. Within the next few days she again slipped into Samuel's suit. She walked to the home of Israel Wood, the local recruiting officer. He did not recognize her. She enlisted in the army as Timothy Thayer, a name she may have made up, thinking it romantic. She gave her home as the nearby town of Carver.

Mr. Wood's mother, an old lady of seventy, knitting by the fireplace, said to her son as Deborah signed the *Articles of Enlist-ment*, "Thayer holds the quill with his finger in that funny posi-tion, like Deborah Sampson." Deborah tried to control her panic, said nothing. Mr. Wood acted as if he had not heard his mother, handed Deborah the bounty money.

That evening she stopped at Sproat Tavern to celebrate her victory and enjoy a drink or two. The rum rushed to her head. She was told later, although she had no memory of it, that she had sung loudly as she sat at the fifteen-foot pine bar and behaved in "a noisy, indecent manner." She recalled creeping back to the Leonard home, returning the suit to Samuel's chest before collapsing in a daze on her feather bed.

When the time came for the newly enlisted soldiers of Mid-dleborough to join their regiment, to the surprise of Israel Wood, Timothy Thayer was not to be found. Mr. Wood remembered what his mother had said about the way Thayer held the quill. He knew Deborah was staying at the Leonard home. He questioned Jenny, who betrayed Deborah by admitting she had helped her dress in Samuel's suit. Deborah was asked to return the bounty money. She did so, pretended she had enlisted as a joke.

She decided the next time she would not make the mistake of enlisting locally. Samuel's parents wrote him of Deborah's "prank," as they called it. He replied he would never again put the suit on his back so they might as well burn it.

Deborah's mother learned of her daughter's wayward act. The next time she saw Deborah she said she did not understand her, that she was an intelligent, sensitive young woman whom a young man with a future wished to marry. She asked what more Deborah wanted out of life. No doubt Deborah thought, without daring to voice it, *Not a life like yours, Mother, left by a husband to take care of eight children, five of whom you had to give away.* Deborah may have unconsciously vowed no man would ever leave *her*, inflicting pain on the helpless children. She recalled many a violent argument between her mother and father. Once she had seen her father strike her mother across the face when he was drunk.

Deborah knew she could not remain, in her own words, "within the confines of the smoke of my own chimney" as her mother had done, dragging out the days "in a prison of listless pursuits, tasteless enjoyments and seething discontents." She believed it more honorable "to be suffocated by the smoke of cannon in a good cause," if suffocate she must. She thought of herself as "possessing an heroic innocence, rather than an heroic courage," feeling not brave but quietly determined.

She felt sad at leaving Deacon Thomas and his wife without a word. They had been kind to her, given her a home when she had none. They must have known, after all the years she spent with them, that she never would settle for the life of a farmer's wife, that her energy, curiosity and spirit would lead her to break away from the austere world of her ancestors.

Deborah wished for more than the groveling, pitiful existence of the woman of that day. She was eager to leave the chimney corner, abandon her down bed for the hard, damp ground where soldiers slept on marches. Her decision was not that of a "momentary freak, a fugitive woman," as she put it to Mann. She was aware of the danger she might well face in "leaping from the solid base of a stone column to a quagmire."

But she had to take that chance. To Deborah, fighting for the freedom of her country was the only way to find freedom for herself.

She wanted very much to write her mother, if only to prove she was alive and well. But she would have to send the letter by messenger once she reached West Point. Her mother would then know where she was and could easily expose her.

Her mother would have to wait for the truth even if, in the meantime, she believed her headstrong daughter dead. Deborah knew her mother would forgive her, she always had, even if she chose to act in a way her mother thought ridiculous for a woman.

THE CRUEL, COLD WINTER

The end of summer brought a time of celebration. An order was delivered on August 29 from General Washington at his Newburgh headquarters, instructing all brigades to take part in what he called a special campaign. The Fourth Massachusetts Regiment, of which Deborah was part, would serve in the first division of the Left Wing under the command of Major General Lord William Alexander Stirling.

A day later additional orders arrived from General Washington. They described the purpose of the campaign. The entire army was to move down the Hudson River from New Windsor, Fishkill,

West Point and adjacent posts to encamp in specially erected tents at Verplanck's Point.

They were not going to fight the British but ceremoniously bid adieu to allies. The soldiers of the French Army encamped at Crompound were scheduled to break camp on September 27 to march off for Boston, where they would embark for France. A continual round of festivities by the allied camps would be held throughout the month of September.

To the roll of drums and piping of fifes, Deborah arose on August 30 at five o'clock in the morning. She packed her haversack and joined the soldiers of the fortress. They boarded barges at the West Point dock for the thirteen-mile trip down the river. Deborah no doubt chuckled in amusement at General Washington's orders, "No woman to be admitted into the boats on any pretense whatever."

The Continental Army erected tents on the plain at Verplanck's with a view south of the river. Behind them on a hill stood the officers' tents, at the very top that of General Washington. Every night at sunset they could hear the British guns at King's Bridge.

The festivities included a series of parades and drills executed by both French and American armies. Each tried to outdo the other in performance. Deborah excelled in drill, as she did at everything she was asked to carry out. As a result, she was one of the hand-picked group of American infantrymen who demonstrated marching and the handling of a musket in an exhibition Count de Rochambeau declared the equal of the finest veteran drills on the continent of Europe.

As she took part in the march Deborah felt love of country and love of Rochambeau in her heart, thinking of her French grandmother, Bathsheba Le Broce Bradford, who had gallantly given up the frivolities of Parisian life to raise thirteen children in the harsh pilgrim's colony of Plymouth, where America's first settlers landed. Deborah remembered how her grandmother had wanted her to be as brave as Joan of Arc and the Deborah of biblical history, and thought she would be very proud of her now.

When she returned to the fortress after the festivities, Deborah found herself enjoying more comfortable living conditions. At night she lay on her straw pallet, listening to the crickets or the far-off mournful bark of a dog. She wondered if she would ever see any of her brothers or the Thomas boys. Occasionally she asked if anyone had heard of them. It seemed impossible they could have left no trace but her question drew blank looks.

The leaves on the point were turning red, orange and yellow, framing the fortress in autumn's vivid shades. With the chill of October winds, most of the men, except those left behind for garrison duty, were ordered to the army cantonment in nearby New Windsor for the winter months.

Again Deborah was on the march, this time to the site selected for the encampment of the Continental Army by Inspector General Baron Von Steuben and Quartermaster General Timothy Pickering. They chose this spot because it offered an ample supply of food, water, forage and timber. It also was protected by the fortress at West Point and the Hudson Highlands from sudden attack.

New Windsor, surrounded in winter by snow-clad mountains with icebound streams, was located at a crossroads where overland routes from New England and the middle and southern states met at opposite sides of the river, as they did at Verplanck's and Stony Point.

The encampment, a site of sixteen hundred acres, contained seven hundred log huts in which slept nine to ten thousand men, troops from New Jersey, Maryland, New Hampshire, Massachusetts and New York. Each hut was divided into two sections with seven or eight soldiers to a section. Because the huts were so crowded, Deborah's company had to build new huts for their own quarters, sheltered meanwhile throughout other huts, sleeping two to a bunk.

Deborah was kept busy with daily drilling, parading and helping in the erection of the new huts. One day as she carried logs from the forest, the wound in her thigh started to ache again. She thought with dread that perhaps a second musket ball was imbedded in it more deeply than the first. If so, the wound would have to heal by itself or it would become infected and she would die. Whatever the cost, she would not risk going to the hospital again and letting the regimental surgeon take a look at it.

Luckily the pain eased and for relaxation she walked two miles to the Hasbrouck House in Newburgh, General Washington's official headquarters and residence. Built in the Dutch style of gray stone, the farmhouse was one-and-a-half stories high with a gamble roof. It was erected in 1725 by Burger Mynders, a blacksmith, and sold to Jonathan Hasbrouck in 1750. Its substantial construction and expansive view up and down the river made it a practical headquarters.

Twenty-one carpenters had renovated the house for General Washington and his wife, Martha. He had sent for her when it looked as though the war would be a lengthy one. The combined living-dining room, in which the general received his military visitors and his guests, was called "the room with the seven doors and one window." The seven doors led to all the other rooms—his private office, his bedchamber, the family room, the kitchen, the bathroom, a storeroom and the cellar. The one window in the room with the seven doors looked across the river. Mrs. Washington used the private family room to receive ladies who called on her.

General Lafayette also was stationed at New Windsor. Deborah saw him and General Washington together from her view at Verplanck's Point during the celebration for the French Army. She had been impressed by the size of General Washington. He stood six feet, three inches, weighed over 209 pounds. His Roman nose gave him an aristocratic, majestic air. He usually wore a grave expression, never lost his dignity and possessed great energy, this man who almost single-handedly led the American troops to a victory that now seemed almost secure.

Deborah later told Herman Mann she understood how a woman could be "captivated at first sight by the fine figure of a man clad in regimentals," enchanted by the glory of a war hero. At the first sight of General Washington, she felt weak, though not a sensual feeling but more "an ecstasy of spirit." Even when General Washington slept, she had the fantasy his soul would be vigilant, a soft footstep in his chambers or tent would rouse him as though the blast of a trumpet.

Deborah's reaction to General Washington was strong indication of her feminine identification and heterosexuality. The commander in chief of the army became a father figure to her. She felt mesmerized in his presence as she had with her father when she was a little girl. Just as her father was protective of his family, down to shooting birds that stole their corn, so Deborah felt General Washington, the father of his country, would guard *her* from being stolen by the British.

General Washington liked to entertain when not planning military strategy or worrying about the health and appearance of his troops. Dinners at the Washington residence were social events. The ladies wore elaborate, colorful dresses. The meal lasted at least two hours, included three courses, each served with claret or Madeira wine. First there was meat and vegetables, accompanied by pickles and cranberries. Then pastries, apples, hickory nuts and walnuts, shelled with a hammer and eaten with little picks. Tea and coffee were offered from a French silver service.

Rumors of impending peace were now heard all through autumn. Great Britain was believed ready to withdraw its troops from America. Preliminary articles of peace between the United States and Great Britain would finally be agreed on in Paris on November 30, 1782, made public by royal proclamation in London on February 14, 1783, three-and-a-half months later.

General Washington's October orders stated: "The readiest way to promote lasting and honorable peace is to be fully prepared vigorously to prosecute war." For the Continental Army "war" still meant attack on the Tories in Westchester.

Deborah was given orders on December 1 to go with a scouting party to the neutral territory near Peekskill Hollow. She had now replaced woolen breeches and a buckskin waistcoat for the linen of summer. Her socks were of heavy wool, no longer cotton. Some of the men tied strips of wool or leather around their lower legs to keep them warm, put dry leaves between their socks and the wool strips as insulation. Winter boots were too expensive, only a few foot soldiers owned a pair.

Marching along a trail south of Peekskill, Deborah's scouting party was suddenly ambushed by Tories on horseback, firing at them as they attacked. Deborah's company fired back, managed to escape without any fatalities or casualties.

Fatigued and freezing, the party stopped to rest at a house owned by a widow whose last name was Hunt. Widow Hunt appeared willing to put them up for a few hours. She sent her slave George for food and drink. Deborah, perhaps out of her feminine intuition, sensed the widow was unfriendly, warned the sergeant, "I don't think the Widow Hunt is telling the truth. I think she's sent George to trap us."

"Let's go," said the sergeant, ordered the twenty soldiers in the scouting party to put on their coats at once, over their and the widow's protests.

As they walked away from the house, they saw George returning, hands empty.

"Where's the food and drink?" the sergeant asked.

George looked puzzled. "What food and drink, suh?"

"Where did you go?" the sergeant demanded.

"Missus Hunt sent me to tell her friends that the rebels were at her house," he said.

"Come with us," ordered the sergeant.

"Yassuh," said George, a smile on his face. It was clear he hated the Widow Hunt.

Suddenly the troops glimpsed a group of Tories three times their number approaching in the distance. Before them lay the deep Croton River. They faced either drowning or being shot by the enemy.

"There's a sand bar in that river you can cross so the water's not over your head," said George.

"Do you know where it is?" asked the sergeant.

"I think so," he answered.

He led them to a shallow spot, suggested, "Try there."

"You come with us," said the sergeant.

Again George smiled, said, "Yassah."

They plunged into the icy water, haversacks over their shoulders, muskets held high above their heads. Deborah, engulfed to her waist, felt her left thigh throb in pain. When she was two-thirds of the way across the river, a sudden strong current carried her off the sand bar. She had never learned to swim and thought she was going to drown, would be at rest forever in a cold, watery tomb.

As she thrashed helplessly about, water over her head and weighted down by the haversack and musket, a soldier standing on the sand bar threw her a rope. Summoning all her strength, she caught the rope. He drew her up onto the sand bar. With great determination she fought her way through the water, managed to reach the opposite shore. The Tories, on horseback, stood across the river looking angrily at the scouting party, now out of range of their musket balls.

The soldiers were practically cakes of ice, their uniforms frozen to them. They found a general store, bought a brandy cask. After they burst its head, the sergeant said to George, "You deserve the first drink for saving us."

"What you goin' to do with me?" he asked.

"Send you back to the Widow Hunt," answered the sergeant.

"Can't I go wid you?" he pleaded.

"I'm afraid not," said the sergeant. "The Widow Hunt wouldn't like it."

George smiled gratefully and said, "At least you're leavin' me alive. That's more than the Widow Hunt meant to leave you."

Deborah thought a female Tory like Widow Hunt worse than a male Tory, felt she was evening the score—not only a Tory but an owner of slaves—by fighting for the freedom of men of all colors.

She knew what it was like to feel a slave. An indentured servant was not much different, except she knew eventually she would get her liberty. She had been fortunate, the family to whom she was indentured did not beat or starve her or make her feel in any way denigrated. Yet she always felt the outsider, as though she were a servant and somehow inferior to the Thomas family.

But now she was nobody's pawn. She had become her own woman paradoxically enough when she found the strength to masquerade as a man. Only in her disguise was she treated as an equal. Men often made women feel stupid, unequal. She recalled at times the look of contempt on her father's face when he addressed her mother. Women, her mother included, were expected to be obsequious and obeisant. Deborah could not, would not, accept such denigration.

She was relieved to find the wound from the second musket ball no longer ached, not even in the chill of a march. For this Deborah was grateful when ordered to confront even colder weather during her first winter as a soldier in the Continental Army.

General Philip Schuyler sent word from Fort Edward, just north of Albany, he needed help at once in subduing the fierce Mohawk Indians, members of the Six Nation Iroquois Confederacy of tribes in upstate New York and Canada. They had murdered many white patriots on the frontiers above Saratoga. Deborah became part of a detachment of one thousand troops sent to the Indian country north of Albany, near the headwaters of the Hudson.

They sailed to Albany, almost one hundred miles north. The winter landscape was cold and forbidding. The country, except for the dark evergreens, lay as though covered by a shroud. Here, rather than aiming at human targets, she thought, the soldiers shot hare and partridge for food.

They headed north, passed Saratoga, the battlefield where Burgoyne had surrendered fifteen hundred troops on October 14, 1777. The success of the patriots at this spot had persuaded the French to enter the war unofficially, furnishing military leaders like Lafayette as well as money and guns. In March 1778, Benjamin Franklin, the colonies' commissioner to France, who had long wooed that country's support, was received at Versailles as the United States became an accredited power and ally of France.

The weather was very cold but sunny all the way to Fort Edward, where the troops arrived on a serene, frosty December morning. There Deborah met General Schuyler, a man considered one of the war's great heroes, fighting the Indians in this wilderness for many years. With a small but brave band of Continental Army soldiers and militia, he was trying to repress the Mohawks murderous assaults on European settlers and to keep peace.

General Schuyler, accompanied by some of his top Indian hunters, led the troops north to Lake George, taking occasional diversions off the road to fortified churches, armed trading posts and the log cabins of settlers, to learn if there had been Indian raids.

Fort George stood on the southern tip of Lake George, a lake of beauty surrounded by lofty mountains "draped in firs," as Deborah told Mann. Thirty-six miles long and two to four miles wide at various spots, it was said to contain as many islands as there were days in the year. The din and havoc of war seemed worlds away from such tranquility. Here, Deborah later recalled, man, "in spite of his warring passions, could for the moment forget his hostility to his species." For a brief while in the beauty and stillness of the lake she was able to forget her own inner war. She wished she could stay on, even though she might have to "subsist on half rations in a wigwam" in the bitter cold, so she could see spring "dissolve the icy fetters of the lake."

At its northern end, Lake George literally fell with one-hundred-foot falls into Lake Champlain. Just past their juncture stood Fort Ticonderoga in a town of the same name. Crown Point was twelve miles north on the edge of the lake, and Mount Independence in Vermont stood half a mile away across the lake. Some of the fortifications at Ticonderoga, where Ethan Allen's "Green Mountain Boys" had overwhelmed the enemy in the first days of the war, were three hundred feet above the lake, seeming almost to overhang it. The fort was part of a chain of fortifications that started at New York City, alternately possessed by the British and then the American armies.

The soldiers at Fort Ticonderoga had just learned from scouts returning from the southwest that Indians had been slaughtering American settlers along the east branch of the Hudson, which divided into a fork in that area. Deborah became part of a force that set out after these Indians, followed by a few horses and what supplies they could carry, primarily tents and blankets. General Schuyler remained at the fort, ill from a rheumatic disorder and gout.

The sunny weather now vanished, a severe snowstorm emerged as they marched into the foothills of the Adirondack Mountains, the highest Deborah had ever seen. She felt lucky to have had a taste of such frost in the winters at Middleborough, pitying the men from Virginia and the Carolinas. The air, unlike the damp sea air of Plymouth, was very dry and the cold seemed more temperate.

She had never been face to face with an Indian or "savage," as the Plymouth settlers called them. But she had heard of the mutilation and cruel deaths the natives inflicted on the white man, sparing neither women nor children. Redface, redcoat or Tory, they all were enemy to her.

They marched through townships and areas few men had ever heard of, not found on maps. The adventurer who built a settlement twenty miles from the river and lake towns acquired the reputation of a hero. Deborah saw some of these log cabins scattered among the lonely miles.

On the first day the guides led the troops to a spot between Lake Charon and Lake Brant. There they found a few wigwams occupied by several squaws, children and one old man.

"Where are your men?" asked a sergeant.

"Hunting," said a squaw. Then she asked, "You look for game or Tories?"

"Both," he said. "Have you seen any scalps lately?"

The Indians shook their heads no, as though well-rehearsed. The soldiers moved off to prepare for a night's encampment near Bradport, an English settlement, as their horses and baggage came into view. They set up patrols, lay down to sleep.

About midnight they were awakened by a sentinel. He pointed to the southwest, said, "From a hill I saw a large glow in the sky, like a fire."

They struck their tents and marched through the snow-wrapped wilderness toward the midnight blaze. By noon the next day, the snowstorm abated and they could distinctly see a large tower of smoke. This was near the town of Johnsburgh in the northwest part of Warren County.

Suddenly out of a thicket, his shoes sinking deep into a foot of snow, a settler wearing no coat, no hat, no gloves, raced toward them. His face was distorted in terror.

"Help! Help!" he shouted.

They followed him as he raced away, leaving the snow crimson with blood dripping from a wound on his neck. They marched half a mile to the top of a small hill where they saw a full view of the devastation below. They rushed down the hill, closing in on the smoking remains of a large log house.

Deborah saw on the threshold the bloody, fallen figure of a woman, hacked to death by tomahawks. The bodies of two small boys, hanging by their heels, dangled from a tree in the front yard. One was dead, a tomahawk buried in his brain. The other had been scalped but still lived, screaming with pain. A sergeant quickly cut him down.

"Where is my little girl?" the father wailed.

A soldier walked into the smouldering ruins of the house. A few minutes later he carried out a small child, shivering with the cold and whimpering, her shoulder gushing with blood from a toma-hawk wound. The soldier told them she had been hiding under a pile of rags.

As he saw his daughter, the father sank into the snow, exhausted by the loss of blood from the tomahawk wound in his neck as well as by the sight of the butchery of his wife and children. The second son had died by this time, unable to survive the scalping.

Deborah felt a surge of sudden fury not only because of the barbaric savages who had slaughtered this innocent family but at the British who had bribed the Indians to commit such wanton atrocity. She would never forget the horror of this still scene in the forest, all white except for the red of the congealed blood of a dead woman and her two sons, and the still-flowing blood of her daughter and husband who survived the deep gashes of the tomahawk.

"Which way did they go?" the sergeant asked the father.

He pointed to another hill within musket shot of the ashes, said, "Over there." The soldiers set out in pursuit of the butchering Indians. As they reached the top of the hill they saw about seventy Indians encamped at the foot, warming themselves around a fire.

At the sight of the troops the Indians stood up, let out a loud war-whoop. The soldiers raced down the hill and their first musket fire killed several Indians. The Indians fired back with guns bought from the British and Tories, wounding three soldiers. But outnumbered three-to-one, the Indians fled into the forests.

The objective of the army was to prevent a single escape. Seeing one light-footed Indian slip through the fire, Deborah valiantly followed in his pursuit, thinking of the three young tomahawked children and their tortured mother. Running more swiftly than she ever did in competing against the Thomas boys, she overtook the Indian. She had not taken the time to reload her piece, so she raised her bayonet, intending to impale him.

He cowered, said in what seemed a strange accent, "Don't kill me. I didn't hurt the white man."

On sudden impulse she yanked open his leather coat. His chest was white, in startling contrast to the deep brown of his face.

"Who are you?" she asked.

"Not Indian," he said. "White man."

"Why are you with them?"

"They capture me when a boy. Paint my face. Make me go on raids."

She took him prisoner, tied his hands behind his back. He later told the soldiers a similar slaughter had been committed several nights before toward the western branch of the Hudson by the same tribe.

Deborah's competent detachment helped capture twenty Indians and kill fifteen. The troops lost not a man, although three were wounded and had to be carried back to Fort Edward. A small group was left to take care of the injured father and daughter and give rites of burial to the slain members of the family. The rest of the party, including Deborah, took a circuitous route to the west where they found, as the captive had informed them, the burnt ruins of two cabins. The snow, over a foot deep, covered any trace of bodies.

They returned to the junction of the east and west branches of the Hudson, about fifteen miles from Fort Edward, then halted until the group left with the father and daughter appeared to report they had taken the two survivors of the massacre to a neighbor's house. The father told them he emigrated from the western part of Massachusetts at the start of the Revolution and with his own hands cultivated thirty acres of land.

In the next few weeks the competent detachment captured seven groups of raiding Indians in successful surprise attacks. Then the cold became too much of an enemy. Deborah discovered one day she left bloody footprints in the frozen snow as her shoes fell apart, cracked by the ice and snow. Her uniform was torn and tattered, the wool pulled to shreds by bushes and undergrowth.

They were all relieved to learn they were ordered back to New

Windsor at the end of January. The troops had fought almost two months in terrain whose frigid beauty could not make up for the rigors of the weather or the daily fear of running into man-eating wolves whose howls they heard at night or hungry bears who might be wakened from their winter slumber.

At Fort Edward Deborah felt vindicated when her detachment was congratulated by General Schuyler for "distinguished bravery." They had not lost a single man. They had captured or killed more than five hundred Indians. Word of their success had spread among the Mohawks, who now seemed less inclined to murder or mutilate the white patriots.

Deborah suffered no injury while on the hazardous expedition. But back in winter headquarters while repairing one of the huts she froze her feet so badly she temporarily lost all her toenails. Then she ran into a problem that disturbed her even more. A severe epidemic had broken out among the soldiers. Each man was ordered to be inoculated if he never had smallpox. She feared she might be asked to undress, should the inoculation be on the buttocks. Once again, in keeping with the family motto "Disgrace is worse than death," she decided she would rather die than risk exposure of her body. She told a lie to the surgeon, saying she had smallpox as a child. She was lucky and escaped contagion, though often exposed to hundreds of men around her falling ill and dying.

In Deborah's absence work had begun at Fort Edward on January 9 on what was called "the Temple." All the regiments shared in the building of this rectangular, one-story structure, 110 feet long and 30 feet wide. It was to be used as a chapel, the first constructed by the Continental Army. Four small side rooms were planned as offices for special meetings, court-martials and the issuing of supplies.

Each company had to provide its share of the building materials, including twenty-one thousand shingles. Twenty-four sergeants and two officers supervised as the soldiers hauled stones on sleds, lay the foundation, framed the timbers. Deborah collected stones for the two chimneys and the foundation. She also helped construct a bench eight feet, four inches long, with two legs and a support in the middle. She worked with nails, a cross-cut saw, an adz and a one-and-a-half inch auger. Her daily reward was a gill of rum plus a half ration of food. She suffered a dislocated ankle when she stumbled and fell while carrying timber. But she felt satisfaction in carrying out a mission her ancestors had completed so expertly, building a place of worship with her own hands.

The persistent rumors of impending peace not only had dulled the national spirit, making it difficult to get food and other supplies for the army, but aroused unrest among the soldiers who believed the British, who had lost two whole armies, were ready to give up. News of French victories in the West Indies, the English loss of Minorea, revolt in India and the siege of Gibraltar strengthened this belief. There was deep discontent at the cantonment because of the inactivity since Yorktown, the months of back pay owed the men, the very cold winter, the inadequate food and clothing and the long absence from family and home.

General Washington faced the same problems that confronted him many a season but which were now more critical: how to supply his men with food and clothing, settle disputes among officers, thwart the greed of civilian contractors, arouse the states from apathy and maintain discipline among the grumbling troops. For two months he had not received enough money to pay for his own meals at headquarters. The Continental Congress seemed unable or unwilling to act swiftly and effectively in providing a stable currency.

Although the soldiers complained, they still respected their commander in chief. When he made inspection visits on horseback to the cantonment, the men threw their hats—those who had hats—into the air, clapping and shouting "Huzzah!" General Washington arranged celebrations as often as possible— Christmas, New Year's, his own birthday. Deborah took part in one celebration on February 6, 1783, just after her return from fighting Indians, as the New Windsor troops held a *feu de joie* to honor the anniversary of the French alliance with the United States. She was part of a long line of soldiers, each firing his musket one after the other, starting at the right end of the line.

Men talked of deserting now that the war seemed almost over. With such a heavy concentration in one small area facing shortages of supplies much thievery occurred. Whipping posts were set up in various sections of the encampment. The sentence for stealing or attempting to desert was one hundred lashes on the naked back, given a soldier caught stealing shirts and blankets from a public store in Newburgh. The whipping was not inflicted all at once but twenty-five lashes at a time in front of four different brigades, as a warning to the other men. Anyone found guilty of trying to incite a mutiny, as several were, was put to death. The soldiers were outraged at what they thought severe penalties.

One night a soldier, sentenced to fifty lashes "on his naked breech" for stealing, cooking and eating a chicken from the army supplies, walked over to Deborah and said he was deserting. He asked if she wanted to go along. She told him she understood how he felt but she could not abandon the fight just as it seemed won, she had enlisted to set her country free and believed it a great disloyalty as well as a sign of cowardice to desert.

After her return from the Indian expedition, many of the men looked at her with admiration as though for a lad who still did not shave, she had earned their respect. They no longer teased her by calling her "Molly" or "blooming smockface." She had learned to answer to the nickname of "Robbie," "Rob," "Bobby" or "Bob." A few called her Robert, her enlistment first name.

She often wondered what the men would say if they knew Robert Shurtliff was actually a woman named Deborah Sampson. It occurred to her in amusement that her last name, minus the "p," spelled Samson. She had indeed become a female Samson, shown strength in her army career in a quiet but impressive way.

With luck still on her side, she hoped she could end her career in the army with no one discovering her duplicity.

8

THE SECRET REVEALED

As the hard winter, one of the most severe in years, finally ended, Deborah's company was ordered to return to West Point. Just before she left a crisis occurred, not in the ranks of the soldiers but among the officers.

Negotiations for peace were taking months to complete. The preliminary articles of peace between Great Britain and the United States could not be declared final until other terms were agreed upon by France, Spain and Great Britain. More than the freedom of America was involved. Issues remained to be settled among the other three countries in their power struggle for territories in America and the West Indies.

Early in the year a committee of officers stationed at New Windsor sent Congress a request for payment of arrears, settlement of food and clothing accounts, a proposed commutation of the pension in exchange for six years' full pay, and assurance of half-pay for life to the incapacitated and retired. Congress had promised them all this three years before in the fall of 1780. Now Congress was refusing to guarantee the promises. A meeting of the general and field officers of the Continental Army was scheduled in Newburgh for March 11, following the circulation of the anonymous "Newburgh Letters" throughout the New Windsor encampment.

The letters were rumored to be the work of Major John Armstrong, aide to General Gates. They attacked the "coldness and severity" of Congress toward the officers' financial distress, urged them should Congress ignore "a last remonstrance," to desert the country during the war, or refuse to lay down arms in the event of peace until their conditions were met.

General Washington was reported as appalled when he read the letters. They implied a revolt against the United States by a leadership that was experienced and intelligent enough to overthrow the weak government. To forestall "disorderly proceedings" he ordered a meeting on March 15, 1783 that all officers were asked to attend, taking the place of the one scheduled for March 11. Its purpose was to determine "what further measures ought to be adopted as the most rational and best calculated to attain the just and important object in view." General Gates, not General Washington, who did not intend to be heard, would preside.

But when another anonymous letter passed from hand to hand expressed the opinion that his call for a meeting sanctified the officers' demands, General Washington decided he would address the meeting. The officers gathered in the newly constructed "temple" Deborah had helped build, to hear their commander in chief speak.

Washington told them, "This dreadful alternative of either deserting our country in the extremest hour of her distress, or turning our arms against it, which is the apparent object, unless Congress can be compelled into instant compliance, has something so shocking in it, that humanity revolts at the idea. My God! what can this writer have in view, in recommending such measures? Can he be a friend to the army? Rather is he not an insidious foe; some emissary, perhaps, from New York, plotting the ruin of both, by sowing the seeds of discord and separation between the civil and military powers of the continent?"

He pledged to do all he could to see the officers' demands were met, citing his own long service to the country and to his army as evidence of loyalty. He defended the integrity of Congress, explaining their deliberations were slow because they had "a variety of different interests to reconcile."

General Washington then drew from his pocket a letter from Joseph Jones, the Virginia delegate to Congress. After reading the first paragraph, which pointed out the difficulties Congress had in taking action and asked that officers be "generously dealt with," General Washington paused.

He then took out his spectacles and apologized. He said he had grown gray in the service of his country and now found himself "growing blind."

He won this battle of wits as he received a vote of thanks and the officers expressed their confidence in Congress. They asked him to act on their behalf, repudiating the proposals of the anonymous letters. Then they quietly adjourned.

Deborah must have admired General Washington even more for so diplomatically averting a revolt that could have been the most dangerous of the war. She probably was amused that, in his obvious horror at the acts of his officers he forgot his admonitions to the soldiers and cursed, taking the name of the Lord in vain as he exclaimed, "My God! What can this writer have in view, in recommending such measures?"

Deborah watched another spring burst the trees and flowers into bloom at the Fortress as the foliage spread out on the cliffs and in the nearby valleys. She planted bean seeds in the company's vegetable garden.

On the first day of April a sergeant walked over to her as she weeded the garden, announced, "General Paterson wants to see you."

A cold chill ran through her veins; this was the first time the general of her brigade had asked her to report to him. She immediately thought, *Someone has suspected I am a woman and General Paterson is going to confront me with this crime and order me executed.*

General Paterson stood six feet, two inches tall. He was the grandson of a Scotsman who emigrated to New England before the 1700s. The general graduated from Yale in 1762, taught school in his hometown of Wethersfield, Connecticut, then practiced law. When news of Lexington and Concord reached him, within eighteen hours he marched with an armed unit for Boston. He took part in the battles of Trenton and Princeton and, on February 21, 1777, was promoted to brigadier general. This loyal patriot then fought in the battle of Saratoga where his horse was shot from under him by a cannon ball, also saw action at Valley Forge. On September 30, 1783, he was appointed major general, the next highest rank to commander in chief.

Expecting to be accused of her unspeakable deed, quaking as she saluted him, Deborah was stunned when he told her that he admired her courage, perseverance and willingness to accept any task, no matter how difficult. He then asked her to serve temporarily as his aide-de-camp, explaining Major Elnathon Haskell, his regular aide-de-camp, had fallen ill.

Deborah, who had expected lashings both verbal and physical

only to receive compliments, commendation and a slight promotion, felt complimented at the general's request. He told her to move at once to his quarters.

Aide-de-camp was a fancy word for orderly. Deborah would now face many menial chores but live in far greater comfort. She moved out of the tent, exchanging her pallet of straw and burlap for a feather bed. Responsible only to General Paterson, her daily routine included cleaning his boots, polishing his swords, making sure he had enough handkerchiefs, preparing some of his favorite dishes and going on errands for him. She was assigned her own horse to take messages from General Paterson to distant towns.

Deborah found it a relief to possess a room of her own even though during her army stint she had never been molested or even approached sexually by a soldier. Perhaps because she never flirted, she told Mann, the men treated her as a virtuous youth who diligently and bravely did his best to serve his country. She never allowed another soldier to put his arm across her shoulder as many a twosome did while walking along the road. Once she was reluctantly drawn into a ring where soldiers took turns wrestling. She was flung to the ground several times but not hurt.

Among the distinguished guests who sometimes visited General Paterson's quarters was a chaplain from Wrentham, Massachusetts, where he was a powerful and popular preacher. During one visit he kept staring at her. General Paterson had told him of the perils of the Indian expedition and praised Deborah's bravery.

The chaplain's eyes kept following her as she prepared the table for supper, then served the beef, potatoes and green beans. Finally he turned to General Paterson and said, "I admire your fare, General Paterson, but even more your very polite attendant, who appears to possess the gracefulness and demeanor of a girl."

Deborah may well have thought, *I could cheerfully kill this chaplain with musket, knife or fork, as easily as I could a Tory.* She was relieved to hear General Paterson say in a serious tone, as though to reprimand the chaplain, "Private Shurtliff is one of my finest men and one of our quiet heroes. Though he may not be as athletic as a General Putnam, he is as expert with a musket as in arraying our table for an attack with knives and forks."

General Paterson sent her on April 18 to Smith's Clove, a cultivated plain at the foot of high mountains fourteen miles west of the fortress. She was ordered to bring back money originally given a farmer for provisions he failed to deliver. She rode her horse, carried her musket. She arrived at Smith's Clove, the farmer repaid what he owed and she wheeled her horse around for the return to West Point.

At twilight she had just recrossed the mountains between Smith's Clove and the fortress. She rode slowly, enjoying the fresh spring air and the wind that caressed her weather-beaten cheeks.

Suddenly two ruffians, handkerchiefs tied over the lower parts of their faces, leaped from behind a rock that projected into the road. One seized the reins of her horse before she had time to put the spur to him and ordered in a muffled tone, "Surrender your money!"

She noticed the thieves carried clubs, not guns. She thought she recognized the man's voice. Seizing her musket, she warned, "If you don't let my horse go, you're a dead man, John Anderson."

The other man fled. Anderson lifted the handkerchief from his face, pleaded, "Don't shoot me."

"If you promise never to try this again," she said. "Otherwise you could be court-martialed and executed."

"I promise," he answered. "If you won't tell anyone I've been so foolish."

"It's a deal," she agreed.

The two men obviously had known she was riding to Smith's Clove for the money and planned to hold her up. She understood their desperation. They, like her, had probably not received one cent of pay in months, perhaps years. She never told anyone about the holdup.

The next day, April 19, proved joyful to the army and all of America. A courier had earlier brought word that a preliminary treaty of peace had been signed by Great Britain, France and Spain. But the formal closing of the war had to wait for the drafting and signing of a definitive treaty.

The new preliminary treaty made operative the November pact between Great Britain and America. And on April 19, 1783, exactly eight years to the day of the Battle of Lexington and Concord, General Washington stood at the door of the "temple" and announced to his army "the cessation of hostilities between the United States of America and the King of Great Britain."

This meant sentinels at the outposts now could amicably exchange a quid of tobacco with their enemies. To all purposes the fighting had ended, though there still would be suspense and uncertainty until the new treaty was ratified.

For Deborah time must have stood still at this point. She had accomplished with honor her original mission, to help win the war. She showed she was as capable as a man on the battlefield and taken vengeance on Great Britain, her hated enemy. She had put to rest the humiliation she suffered when she was four-and-a-half at the hands of her Uncle Simeon, proving him wrong. She had also, in fighting men, eased her buried rage at her father for abandoning her. She felt justified pride in her achievements.

Deborah realized the end of war undoubtedly would bring new problems. She wondered how her family would react when she returned home. Would they speak to her or ostracize her? Would her mother still love her or hate her, believing she had committed a crime in disguising herself as a man? Could the Church possibly accept in good faith a young woman whose violation of a principle the Church might view with horror? She did not know if she would return to a joyful reunion or be banned from the state of Massachusetts.

Most of all she worried about reentry into her past work. She had worn men's clothing for almost a year-and-a-half. If she taught school she would be compelled to wear women's dresses. Would she miss the freedom and lack of constriction found in men's trousers? With her weather-beaten face and roughened hands would she seem attractive to a man? And yet, despite these worries, part of her felt secret relief at the idea of once again being her feminine self.

She knew she faced many thoughts to work out before going home. The hiatus between war and peace would serve her well.

When Major Haskell returned in good health to work as General Paterson's aide-de-camp, Deborah reluctantly moved to her tent. The men teased her about the sudden "demotion" but seemed happy to have her back—especially those who could not sew or write.

Scouting party trips into the neutral territory came to an end with the cessation of hostilities, although the British still occupied New York. But now another sort of fighting faced Deborah. A kind she never had anticipated, not even in her nightmares.

To finance the war, Congress had resorted to loans from foreign countries, chiefly France, issuing large quantities of paper money. The continental currency had depreciated so rapidly it was now practically worthless. Congress had neither the funds to pay the troops or the power to raise taxes. General Washington averted a rebellion as he had done with the officers by promising action on the troops' behalf. Most of the soldiers were content to wait.

But eighty troops encamped at Lancaster, Pennsylvania, rose in revolt. They marched sixty-seven miles to Philadelphia where Congress was in session to demand back pay. Arriving on June 29, they were joined by two hundred troops from the Carolinas.

Armed with artillery seized from the Philadelphia barracks they marched, drums beating, on the State House. They sent in a message to Congress announcing that if their demands were not met in twenty minutes they would storm the meeting.

The members of Congress succeeded in escaping out the back doors, sent word of the mutiny to General Washington. He at once ordered a detachment of fifteen hundred soldiers from West Point under the command of Major General Robert Howe to proceed to Philadelphia and suppress the mutiny. In the spirit of patriotism, Deborah was eager to be part of that detachment.

But to her chagrin the horse assigned her was lame and had to rest. She was unable to leave West Point until four days after General Howe departed with the main contingent. She rode with four officers through the marshes and hills of New Jersey, past the battlefields of Newark and Trenton, on to Philadelphia. Her thigh wound, which she thought was healed, started to bleed from the pressure of riding horseback that distance. At a tavern she bandaged it with a piece of linen she carried in her haversack in preparation for the monthly flow of blood.

As she approached the City of Brotherly Love, she may have thought of the mutinous soldiers and the fact that she had never received one penny beyond the bounty money given by the town of Uxbridge. But she had not cared about money, only wished to be accepted by the army, fed, sheltered, clothed and given the chance to fight for her country. She later told Mann she thought it enough that America's hills and valleys had "been whitening with the bones of our soldiers" for eight years, that it would be tragic to see a civil war grow out of a foreign one if men, whose swords had "cut the cords of tyranny" were now "raised to rip open the intestines of their brothers."

By the time her small group reached Philadelphia the mutiny had ended. When General Howe arrived the insurgents had given up their arms. The ringleaders were tried. Two were sentenced to death and four to imprisonment. Congress later pardoned them all.

Deborah caught up with the rest of the detachment encamped on a hill that offered a spectacular view of America's largest metropolis, including a mass of church spires rising above red-tiled roofs. She lost no time exploring the city she had long wished to see.

She visited Carpenters Hall where the Declaration of Independence was signed 284 years after Columbus discovered America and 156 years after her ancestors settled in Plymouth. It was also at Carpenter's Hall that the first Continental Congress met on September 5, 1774 for seven weeks in response to Boston's plea that the colonies unite. Paul Revere had ridden as messenger once again, this time from Boston to Philadelphia on behalf of The Committees of Correspondence in Massachusetts. His message called for a Solemn League and Covenant asking the colonies to cease trading with England until the act closing the port of Boston was repealed. Congress responded with its Declaration of Rights. This included the provision there would be no more importing or consumption of British goods after December 1, 1774, but delayed the ban on exporting goods to Britain, except for rice (to placate the Southern colonies) until September 1, 1775.

There was no difficulty now importing or exporting, for the wharves of the busiest trading port in America were heaped with products from all the colonies—beaver pelts, tobacco, pigs, sheep, venison, deer, bear meat, deer hides by the thousands and white pine floated down the Delaware.

Philadelphia was a cultural center, with its large library and headquarters of the American Philosophical Society founded by Benjamin Franklin in 1769 to promote knowledge of applied science and practical arts. There also was the Pennsylvania Hospital, the first public hospital in the country (Boston as yet had no hospitals). There were countless taverns and coffee houses, shops filled with delicacies, expensive clothing and furniture created by patriot carpenters, not Chippendale or Sheaton but American, simple and sturdy.

Deborah had long wished to explore historical Philadelphia. For the girl soldier from the farm in Middleborough the Philadelphia scenes were overwhelming. She saw the mixture of many nations—of the British, of the wooden-shoes Dutchmen who brought their produce-filled flatboats from New Jersey, of tall Swedes from the Delaware country, of Indians wrapped in blankets from the mountains of Virginia and of Africans brought to be sold as slaves.

Everyone walked in the spirit of peace, smiles on their faces instead of fear and taut expressions. Deborah no longer was afraid of death from a musket ball or saber wielded by redcoat, Tory or Indian. Then she discovered a new enemy. One that was to fell her as the British never could.

An epidemic of malignant fever suddenly raged among the soldiers. One night at the encampment on the hill Deborah started to shiver with the cold, as though it were the dead of winter, not the first of July. She also felt as if a burning iron pressed across her forehead. Then she lost consciousness. She later learned several men in her company had carried her to the Pennsylvania Hospital.

She regained awareness to find herself lying on the floor of a hospital. She saw the corpse of a soldier removed from the bunk next to her, then felt herself lifted from the floor and placed on the bunk vacated by the dead soldier. She fainted again.

When she came to a second time she heard a man's voice say, as he pointed to her, "I'll take this one's breeches before we send him to Potter's Field." This was the city cemetery for the poor.

"No fair," protested another voice. "You took the breeches off the last chap."

She realized in terror she was about to be buried alive. Making a superhuman effort, she pulled at the coat of a male nurse as he raced by. She pleaded in a whisper, "Don't let them bury me."

He turned on the two undertakers, snarled, "Get out of here, you vultures! Can't you even wait till they die?"

A woman Deborah later learned was the hospital matron, majestically approached her bunk as the male nurse said, "This man is still breathing."

The next thing Deborah knew a doctor stood beside her. She heard him call her by name, "Private Shurtliff," and ask, "Can you speak?"

She tried to reach him through the fog of her fever but nothing emerged from her mouth. She saw him turn away as though he were giving up all hope, leaving her for dead.

With what she felt her last breath, she struggled to appeal to him. All she could manage was a gurgle. But it was enough.

She saw him turn back to her, walk swiftly to her side, evidently moved by the primitive sound she had uttered. He started to thrust his hand into her bosom to find out if her heart were still beating.

There was no way she could stop him. She did not have the strength. He hastily ripped away her waistcoat and shirt, exposing the white linen strip that bound her breasts. She saw a startled look on his face. He hesitated a moment, raised her a few inches off the bunk, then gently unwound the linen strip.

As she lay, breasts bared, she saw shock in his eyes. But he said not a word. He bent over and listened to her heartbeat. Then, slowly, thoughtfully, he took down her breeches, uncovering the bandage she had placed over her thigh. He lifted it, examined the wound. He put salve on it and a new bandage of lint.

Deborah kept her eyes tightly closed in shame and embarrassment, her naked body exposed to his gaze. Her face flushed, her ears felt on fire. She wanted to cross her hands protectively over her lower parts but felt paralyzed, mortified, humiliated. Once again the little girl of four-and-a-half who wanted to do what a boy could do when she had been rejected by her Uncle Simeon. The moment seemed stuck in time, as if it would tarry forever.

Yet underneath the surface flared a spark of excitement, a new freedom. Someone now knew her buried secret. She felt a deep relief, she would no longer have to guard the crime she feared might be exposed.

The doctor helped her put back the white linen strip, shirt, waistcoat and breeches. Then he forced a vile-tasting medicine down her throat. In a few minutes she again felt blood flow through her veins.

She heard him say to the matron, "This young soldier is a woman disguised as a man. Take her to your apartment and care for her as though she were your daughter. Please be discreet. No one knows her secret."

Deborah was thankful that at least for the moment she was safe. Two male nurses carried her into the apartment at the hospital where the matron lived. For the next few days the kindly matron took care of Deborah. When her fever dropped to normal the two male nurses again appeared, lifted her off the bed, carried her to a carriage standing outside the hospital.

"Where are you taking me?" she asked worriedly, fearing to the jail where she would await punishment befitting her crime of pretending to be a man.

"To Dr. Binney's home," one of the men answered.

"Who is Dr. Binney?" she asked.

"The surgeon of the hospital. Dr. Barnabus Binney. The doctor who treated you."

They rode through the Philadelphia streets, eventually stopped at a large brick house set among tall trees and flowering bushes. The two men carried Deborah up the steps and into the parlor. Dr. Binney was not at home but his wife solicitously asked the male nurses to bring Deborah upstairs, place her on a bed in the spare room.

After the men left Mrs. Binney fed Deborah soup and crackers, addressed her as Private Shurtliff, treated her as a gallant patriot soldier saved from the jaws of the deadly flu.

That evening when Dr. Binney returned home he walked into the room where Deborah lay, felt her forehead. He told her the fever had vanished but she had to be slowly nursed back to health.

She lay quivering, expected him to castigate her but he said not a word about his astounding discovery. He only asked, "Where is your home?"

"Middleborough, Massachusetts," she answered.

He smiled, said, "My home is Boston and I miss it." Then asked, "How long have you been in the army?"

"One year and almost two months," she said.

"Have you seen much action?" He sounded curious.

"Quite a bit in the neutral territory of New York, fighting Tories and also Indians in the Adirondacks."

He warned, "Don't expect too much of yourself in the next few weeks. You have had a very rough time of it with this flu. We just about pulled you through an exceptionally high fever."

"I don't think I'll ever be able to thank you enough," she said.

"Just get well." He smiled again, then was gone.

She wanted to ask if he were going to give away her secret, but did not dare. One always waited for the doctor to speak, she had been taught growing up.

It seemed weeks before her energy returned. One morning she awoke to find a delicately featured young woman bringing in breakfast. The young woman explained she was Dr. Binney's niece, an orphan who lived in Baltimore but traveled to Philadelphia to help her aunt take care of Deborah.

The niece sat for hours by Deborah's bedside, bathed her face, brought her flowers. Deborah realized the young girl was falling in love with Robert Shurtliff, visualizing him as an eighteenth century Sir Galahad who had single-handedly freed the colonies from British enslavement. Deborah felt remorse and self-reproach. Evidently Dr. Binney had told no one except the hospital matron that Private Shurtliff was a woman.

Deborah did not wish to inflict pain on a young woman to whom she felt deep gratitude. But she did not know how to extricate herself from the situation—or the social functions the young woman and Mrs. Binney thrust upon her when she recovered, pleading they needed a masculine escort, as Dr. Binney was always too busy or too exhausted to go out.

She found herself accompanying the two women on sails down the Delaware River, elaborate parties where the élite of Philadelphia drank claret, Madeira and port served out of silver punch bowls. She consumed dozens of varieties of cold meats, creamy frosted cakes and cookies. After the army fare on which Deborah had subsisted, she stared in wonder, almost disbelief, at the well-laden tables. The women wore satin and velvet dresses, brocaded, silvered or gilded, trimmed with layers of lace. The men's suits were also of expensive, elegant fabrics, their hair was powdered, covered with a wig.

The niece, who told Deborah she had inherited money from her parents, handed her a present of three expensive men's shirts, as young girls often did the soldiers they loved. At that moment Deborah almost confessed Robert Shurtliff was a woman. Then she thought, *If Dr. Binney has not told his wife and niece the truth he must have a reason and I will not give away my secret either but bless him eternally for keeping it.*

Deborah constantly wondered why Dr. Binney had not publicly revealed her masquerade, since he had told the matron the truth. She thought the reason must be that he was convinced she did not know of his discovery, believing she was unconscious when he made it.

Deborah thanked the niece for her generosity and kindness in taking care of her. She said she wished there were some way she could repay her but she had to return at once to her regiment. Deborah vowed one day she would tell the niece the truth so she would not feel hurt because her love had been rejected. Deborah understood the pain of unrequited love. She did not want the young woman to suffer as she had when her father, her first and only love thus far, had left his family to go to sea, never returned.

Deborah thought it ironic that a member of her own sex had fallen in love with her whereas those of the opposite sex never even realized she was a woman. Because of the niece's feelings, Deborah planned to return to the army immediately. She asked Dr. Binney if she could speak to him alone.

He invited her into his library where books lined two whole walls. As they sat facing each other he looked at her with deep concern, as he had in the hospital.

Then he asked, "Do you have any friend in the army? Someone in whom you can confide?"

"No," she said.

She had never possessed a close friend. She had always been alone, ever since the day her mother turned her over to Cousin Ruth Fuller. She prided herself on not needing anyone, she could take care of herself quite adequately. It never occurred to Deborah that she distanced herself from both men and women to shield from everyone the secret longings of her heart.

"What are you going to do now?" Dr. Binney asked.

"Go back to my detachment on the hill," she said, adding, "if they're still there."

"They've broken camp and returned to West Point," he informed her.

"I guess they think I died from the flu," she said.

She had not thought they might leave her behind. The two soldiers who had taken her to the hospital evidently took it for granted she had expired when they did not hear from her.

"I know the way back," she said. "I'll find a horse and ride to West Point, like I came down."

She added wistfully, "Though, since I'm this far south, I'd like to see more of the country. I may never get another chance. But it's only a dream because I haven't any money. We haven't been paid in over a year."

Dr. Binney looked at her thoughtfully, then said, "I have a very good idea. You've been fighting without pay to protect us all. Your superior officers believe you're dead of malignant fever and couldn't care less. Time enough to go back to West Point. I have a friend, Colonel Benjamin Tupper, looking for soldiers to accompany him into unexplored territory in Virginia to make geological and mineralogical surveys. He wants the protection of the soldier's rifle in case he comes across Indians who might seek his scalp. Would you like to go with him and see the wild west?"

He added, "Colonel Tupper will gladly pay all your expenses."

"Are you sure he will take me?" she asked. The opportunity seemed too exciting to be missed.

"I'll arrange everything," Dr. Binney said. (She would later learn Dr. Binney not only took care of everything, but also paid for her trip, a way of thanking her for fighting on behalf of the colonies.)

She felt relieved the doctor was not going to question her further. She realized he understood more than anyone ever had, and probably more than anyone ever would, her desire to masquerade as a man in the interests of her country. He also knew how much she would enjoy seeing more of that country before she settled down for life on a Massachusetts farm to raise a family.

"I want you to promise me one thing," he said.

"What's that, Dr. Binney?" She felt uneasy; would he ask her to dress as a woman?

"That you will stop in to see me when you return here with Colonel Tupper. This is important," he insisted.

"Of course. I wouldn't think of leaving Philadelphia without thanking you again for saving my life." She left unsaid that he had saved her life in more ways than one, not only from the life-threatening fever but in not telling the army of her deceitful act.

"It was a pleasure to save the life of one so deserving," he said solemnly.

Then he asked, almost hesitantly, "Could you tell me both your real and assumed names?"

"My real name is Deborah Sampson," she said, "and I took the first two parts of my brother's name, Robert Shurtliff, the first-born of my mother's eight children. He died when he was eight, the year I was born. I never saw him but I knew my mother never got over her grief at his loss."

Dr. Binney stood up. He walked over to Deborah, grasped her right hand. He said, "You are a brave young woman, Deborah Sampson. Your name will go down in history."

She blushed, said, "I hope no one finds out what I did."

"Don't be ashamed of it," he advised. "You fought to save your country from the invading British."

It seemed understood he would keep her secret. She did not

know why but she trusted him completely as she had never trusted anyone. He appeared to admire her, not wish to punish her. For this she would be eternally grateful. He did not believe she was a criminal but praised her daring on behalf of the colonies.

His last words were, "Enjoy the trip with Dr. Tupper."

The fireplace in the room where Deborah Sampson was born on December 17, 1760, at 46 Elm Street, Plympton, Massachusetts. This photo shows the original setting in what was described as "the borning room."

The main fireplace in the Deborah Sampson house, in which eight children—five sons and three daughters—were delivered. Deborah was the second daughter.

The sign that still denotes the spot where Deborah was born. The house was sold several times, modernized by each buyer.

BIRTH-PLACE
OF
DEBORAH SAMPSON

The Deborah Sampson house as it looked in 1900 after several families had lived there. In the distance can be seen the barn that one of the families built.

The Deborah Sampson house as it looked during this century, remodeled with a large garage added to it. Deborah would not have recognized her earliest home.

This was Deborah's home from the age of ten until eighteen when she became "an indentured servant," living with the Reverend Benjamin Thomas, his wife, and ten sons. The latter taught her how to use a gun to shoot down birds destroying the crops.

The town of Plympton as it appeared on the cover of Tales of Old Plympton *describing "our New England heritage," according to the Plympton Historical Society, which put the book together in stories that "capture the essence of the town as it was before modernization began." It was written by Eugene Wright.*

Plympton
Massachusetts

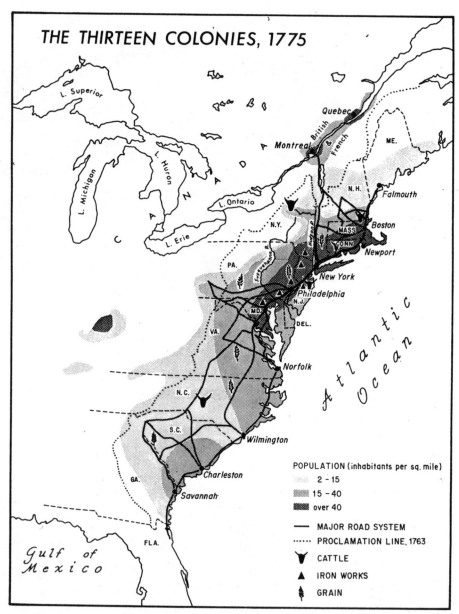

THE THIRTEEN COLONIES, 1775

L. Superior

L. Michigan

L. Huron

L. Erie

L. Ontario

C A N A D A

British & French

Quebec

Montreal

ME.

N.H.

Falmouth

N.Y.

MASS.

Boston

CONN.

Newport

New York

PA.

Philadelphia

N.J.

MD.

DEL.

VA.

Norfolk

Atlantic Ocean

N.C.

S.C.

Wilmington

GA.

Charleston

Savannah

FLA.

Gulf of Mexico

POPULATION (inhabitants per sq. mile)

▨ 2 – 15

▨ 15 – 40

■ over 40

—— MAJOR ROAD SYSTEM

······ PROCLAMATION LINE, 1763

⛉ CATTLE

▲ IRON WORKS

⚘ GRAIN

A map of what was then the thirteen colonies in 1775 and the major "road system," with pictures of where cattle, iron works, and grain existed. Deborah would be fighting in the war seven years later.

This is the scene of part of the Hudson Highlands where West Point defenses appeared in 1780, two years before Deborah would be fighting there.

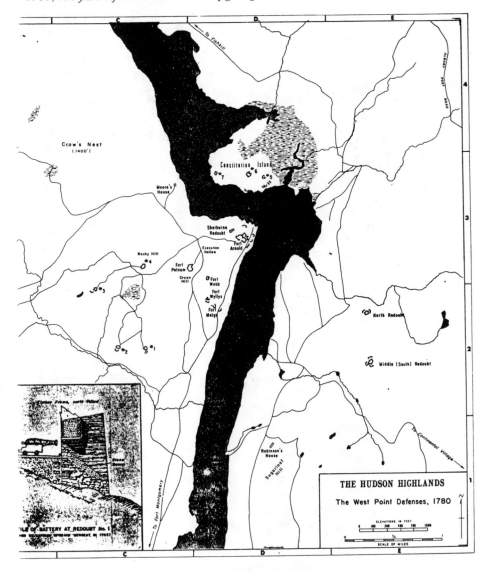

THE HUDSON HIGHLANDS

The West Point Defenses, 1780

A picture of Deborah drawn by Joseph
Stone of Framingham, Massachusetts, for
the frontispiece of a book about her war
experiences. Called The Female Review,
Memories of an American Young
Lady, it was written in 1797 by
Herman Mann, printer and editorial
writer for The Village Register in
Dedham, Massachusetts.

DEBORAH SAMPSON.
Published by H. Mann. 1797.

Another
portrait of
Deborah
painted by
Joseph Stone for
Mann's book.
Her face is
somewhat
different in
this painting,
as is the
decoration at
the top of the
frame.

DEBORAH SAMPSON
Drawn by Joseph Stone Framingham 1797

A water color painting of
Deborah Sampson by
Herbert Knotel, courtesy of
the West Point Museum
Collections. It hangs in the
West Point Museum.

This rather idealized likeness of Deborah appeared in 1987 on a newly designed Plympton fireman's shoulder patch. She supposedly held the gun that carried her through a year and a half of warfare.

This was the notice of Deborah's second appearance on the stage in Boston as she appeared "in complete uniform" to address the audience. She would "go through the manual exercise," complete with gun, as she described her experiences in the war.

Theatre --- Federal Street.

THE PUBLIC

Are respectively informed, that Mrs. GANNETT, (late Deborah Sampson,) the AMERICAN HEROINE, who served three years as a private Soldier in the Continental Army, during the War, will at the request of a number of respectable persons, make her second appearance on the Stage TO-MORROW EVENING, for the purpose of relating her Narrative, &c.

TO-MORROW EVENING, March 24, Will be presented, (by particular desire) for the second time these two years, the much admired Historical Play, in 5 acts, called,

KING HENRY the IVth,

With the Humors of Sir JOHN FALSTAFF.
Characters as before.

To which will be added, by way of Farce, an Olio, consisting of Song, Sentiment, &c called,

THE SOLDIER's FESTIVAL ;
ON THE EVE OF BATTLE.

1st. In the course of which Mrs. GANNETT will deliver her narrative.
2d. Glee--"How Merrily we live that Soldiers be."
3d Song--"How stands the Glass around."
4th Glee--"Here's a health to all true Lasses."
5th Glee--"How shall we mortals spend our hours.'

Mrs. Gannett,
Equipt in complete uniform will go through the MANUAL EXERCISE.
The whole to conclude with the Song and Chorus of
" God Save the Sixteen States."

Deborah's tombstone in Rock Ridge Cemetery, Sharon, Massachusetts, reads, "Deborah, wife of Benjamin Gannett, died April 29, 1827, age sixty-eight years." She lies today between the graves of her husband and son. The other side of the gravestone holds the inscription "Deborah Sampson Gannett, Robert Shurtleff, The Female Soldier. Service (1781–1783)."

Deborah was honored in a plaque describing her as "Revolutionary Soldier—1775–1783." It was placed in her birthplace, Plympton, by the Deborah Sampson Chapter of the Daughters of the American Revolution.

A second plaque was erected in 1906 by the Daughters of the American Revolution of Brockton and the town of Plympton, "In honor of Deborah Sampson, who for love of country served two years as a soldier in the WAR OF THE REVOLUTION." It held her birth date in Plympton, "December 17, 1760."

WESTWARD TO THE OHIO RIVER

Deborah achieved one of her major goals in enlisting in the army—she succeeded in traveling as her father had done. She saw the wilderness of upper New York State. She journeyed on horseback through the hills and valleys of New Jersey and Pennsylvania on her way to Philadelphia. Now she was bound for Virginia's uncharted territory, headed as far west as the unexplored Ohio River. If the colonies were too poor or too corrupt to pay for her military service, the travel she would enjoy at Dr. Binney's expense was ample reward.

She felt at ease with Colonel Tupper, a cordial man whose home was in Sharon, Massachusetts, not far from where she was born. She liked the spirit of adventure that propelled him into wild country seeking mineral deposits, felt a kinship with him. He also brought back thoughts of her father, another kind of explorer.

The colonel was equipped with a pack of hunting dogs and hazel-rods to locate minerals in the ground. He willingly accepted Robert Shurtliff as a member of his small expedition on Dr. Binney's recommendation. The six members of the group included five soldiers, of which Deborah was one. They were supposed to hold off any enemy, referring to the Indians on whose land they would trespass.

They set out on the journey in mid-September, expecting to be gone about six weeks. Traveling by Conestoga wagon, they reached Baltimore on the first day, then Alexandria, where they sailed down the Potomac in the early morning light. As the sun glistened on a lofty dome high on a hill, Deborah felt a rush of joy when she heard Colonel Tupper announce, "This is Mount Vernon. Let's stop and visit it for a while."

The thought of trodding on hallowed ground that held the birthplace of her contemporary hero, General Washington, appealed to her. He had proved an exemplary father figure, starved as Deborah was for a father's existence. She had admired the general from afar ever since she first heard of his compassion for soldiers and his bravery. She sensed qualities in him that would soon make him famous as "the father of his country."

As in a dream, she followed Colonel Tupper and the other men as they walked up the natural slopes until they reached a plateau. There she saw the ninety-six-foot mansion supported by eight Corinthian columns, which she had described to her school children. She explored the spacious gardens with their serpentine gravel paths, bordered by weeping willows and expansive fruit trees. She marveled at the elaborate home, the greenhouse, the quarters for the officers and slaves, the stables for racehorses and kennels for hunting dogs. It all resembled "a rural village rather than one man's estate," she later told Mann. Her joy was complete when she discovered deer and birds of beautiful plumage in a small park.

Deborah was reluctant to leave a dream made real but envisioned further fantasies that might possibly come true. The party of six traveled three days to the west in a stage coach. At nightfall they were forced to resort to foot when dropped near the bank of a large river enveloped in a thick fog. They enlivened the darkness by a fierce debate as to whether the river was the Monongahela or the Ohio. It turned out both sides were wrong.

Monongahela, Ohio or any other river, the group had no choice but to camp on the bank and wait for the fog to lift. But instead of clearing, the fog grew more dense. The men tried to keep up their spirits singing and joking.

They suddenly heard the roll of distant thunder. Soon, shafts of lightning flashed nearby, followed by thunder crashing down almost on top of their heads. It was the most violent storm Deborah had ever seen, she thought it a tempest that exceeded in sound and fury "all the artillery man could bring together on one battlefield."

Weary, wet and frightened, the group tried to sleep on the leeward side of a shelved rock that screened them somewhat from the rain and winds that raged all night. Still they remained soaked and freezing.

Suddenly one of the hunting dogs that lay between Deborah and another soldier was hit by a bolt of lightning, which then struck a large tree, splitting it into fragments. Deborah felt shocked to realize the bolt had missed her by only half a foot. Visions of her father's storm at sea washed over her. Once again she had narrowly missed joining him in a watery grave, as she thought she might while fleeing the Tories near Peekskill. She would at times recall this scene of thunder and lightning the rest of her life.

In the calm of the next day the soldiers discharged their pieces to clean them. But the peaceful interlude did not last long. The sound of their shots brought a group of Indians in warlike dress out into the open. Colonel Tupper quickly assured the Indian chief his soldiers were friendly, he was searching for precious minerals, not Indians.

The chief did not appear convinced, as Deborah later told Mann. He stared at the colonel impassively. Finally he pointed to one of Colonel Tupper's men, the guide, ordered, "Follow me." Understandably, the guide seemed reluctant to accompany the Indians by himself.

Deborah stepped forward, musket in hand. "I'll go," she offered.

"You don't have to, Private Shurtliff," Colonel Tupper said.

"I want to, sir." She shouldered her musket.

She thought these Indians looked far more friendly than the Mohawks of northern New York, out to murder all white men. She then wondered if there lurked within her a death wish, pulling her to join her father. She thought, *So far, so good.* She had survived the death-dealing flu and was willing to risk these Indians.

The chief seemed impressed by her offer. As though to salute her bravery, he shot an arrow over her head with as true an aim, she thought, as William Tell when he shot the apple from his son's head. Then the Indian took a girdle of wampum, twined it about her waist, ordered, "Follow!" As if to protect her, one of the hunting dogs left the pack to trot by her side. Lonely for the animals of the farm with whom she had grown up, Deborah was delighted to have his company.

The Indians led her about a quarter of a mile to a cave in the woods, ordered her to enter. For the first time she felt fear, thinking perhaps they intended to tomahawk her. But she defiantly marched inside, with all the bravado of her twenty-three years. The Indians advanced to the center of the cave, then fell to the ground, shouting what sounded to her like war cries.

She found herself trembling, wondered if they were preparing to sacrifice her at the stake, like her predecessor, Joan of Arc. To still her shaking hands, she patted the head of the dog, still faithfully by her side.

She was puzzled to see the Indians slowly rise, run deep into the cave and drag forth the bodies of three of their dead. Dare she relax as yet? she wondered. She followed them as they carried the bodies out of the cave, motioning her to follow. They then turned the faces of the dead Indians to the earth. Climbing onto a rocky ledge, they hurled huge boulders far below, emitting war whoops. They pointed to the sky, then the boulders, then the dead Indians.

She understood they were trying to tell her that the three Indians had been killed not by white men but by bolts of lightning in the storm of the preceding evening. She said to the chief, pointing to the dog, "One like this was killed by lightning too."

Satisfied Deborah now knew the cause of the catastrophe, and that she too had suffered because of it, the Indians led her back to her expedition. The men greeted her joyfully, as if they never expected to see Private Shurtliff alive again.

Colonel Tupper corroborated her original fear. He said, "When we heard the war whoops we thought they were scalping you."

The Indian chief solidified their newfound friendship by inviting members of the expedition to funeral ceremonies for the three dead tribesmen. Colonel Tupper reciprocated by hiring two of the Indians as guides to take them over the Allegheny mountains. Deborah found it hopeful that former adversaries could learn to shake hands in friendship, felt proud of the small part she had played in overcoming hostilities.

They found out the name of the river. It was the Shenandoah. It coursed two hundred miles north through rich country, captured between two high ridges of the Allegheny Mountains, a range of the Appalachians that wound through central Pennsylvania, Maryland, West Virginia and Virginia. Making a right angle, the

Shenandoah formed a junction with the Potomac in a scene of virgin splendor, as giant waterfalls crashed against mammoth river rocks.

The Indian guides led them to the Blue Ridge, then the even loftier Allegheny Ridge. They stood on what Colonel Tupper called the ridgepole, the backbone of the United States. The mountains started at the mouth of the St. Lawrence River and in almost unbroken chain rose in majesty all the way south.

Deborah watched rills and rivers spurt from the sides and base of mountains and flow in all directions—east to the ocean, west to the Ohio and Mississippi rivers. The scene was translucent with the light of early morning. She wanted to stop and drink in its glory but had to keep up with the pounding hooves of the expedition.

As she continued onward, she felt she had waited all her life for this ephemeral instant of beauty. They passed a vast canyon ranging from twenty to fifty miles wide, walled by mighty ridges. Fields and forests were dyed with deep autumnal colors—wines, rusts, yellows and greens vied for supremacy in a cacophony of splendor. Overwhelmed with the exquisite beauty, Deborah bowed her head as if in worship at a majestic cathedral. The young guides made the experience as enjoyable as walking in the woods with her brothers or the Thomas boys.

The party suffered a sad experience at the Laurel or Dry Ridge. They came upon a group of trees whose fruits resembled the nectarine. Delighted with the sweet taste, they greedily fell upon the fruit, devoured it. Then they noticed the two Indian guides were not eating any fruit. They shortly discovered why when all the soldiers became sick. Deborah vomited, her nose bled and her stomach ached so she could not move. One of the Indians found special roots which he applied to her nose and each side of her neck. Miraculously, this stopped the pain and the nosebleed. Her appetite for nectarines now also ceased.

About ten miles to the west, the group reached the Mononga-hela River, not far from its first spring. Running north, this river joined the Allegheny River at Pittsburgh, constituting the head and principal branch of the Ohio River. Deborah was receiving a lesson in geography she never could have acquired from books.

According to Colonel Tupper's records, the group passed over the soundings of a number of buried mineral kingdoms. At some spots the hazel-rods trembled and alternately pointed in every direction, as though going mad. Colonel Tupper made the marks and set the seals, predicting one day he would return to lay open treasures of silver and gold.

That night the soldiers argued whether an inexhaustible mine of silver and gold would produce a moral and scientific improvement of a free people more than any general habit of industry and economy. As neither side would yield, they agreed to make an umpire of the first Indian they met. This strange man proclaimed, "A long hunt and a good fish is better than wampum," giving his preference to industry and economy. Deborah tended to agree.

As the group visited an Indian tribe near a settlement called Medikar, suddenly Deborah became so sick she collapsed on the ground. Her head felt on fire, as when she first caught malignant fever.

Colonel Tupper examined her, to her despair announced, "You have a relapse of the fever."

Deborah silently worried, *Will I miss out on the rest of the expedition? If I go to a hospital again and risk discovery, I may not be so fortunate as to find another Dr. Binney.*

But to her great relief the Colonel asked the Indian chief, "Will you take care of Private Shurtliff until we come back at the close of the moon?"

She held her breath as the chief seemed reluctant to take her with them. But the two Indian guides, who apparently enjoyed the company of a young person near their age, pleaded with the chief to allow her to remain so she could recover. They convinced him the white men were neither spies nor invaders seeking to drive the Indian from his wigwam, corn field and hunting ground but only men like themselves who wished peace.

Deborah relaxed somewhat when the chief finally assented. He ordered one Indian and his squaw to care for her, telling them in what Deborah hoped was a jocular tone, "The boy will be good to eat when fat."

She hoped he said this to test her courage. She was too sick to care. After the fruit episode she believed Indian medicine would cure her faster than the medicine of white doctors. Her faith was rewarded when in a few days she once again felt normal.

Deborah had learned much about Indians by now. They cared for her physically even though the chief tortured her with subtle threats of death—teasing her as her brothers once did. When a new chief was shortly installed, he proved no different. He seized her by the shoulder and ushered her into the vast circled assemblage with a ceremony that would have done justice, she thought, to a *petit maître* at a white man's ball. Pointing to kettles of boiling water he said, "I'm going to have a slice of you for dinner."

Years of dealing with her brothers and the boys on the farm had taught Deborah how to handle the chief. She decided to make light of his threat, asked seriously, "Do you prefer Englishmen to venison?"

"Englishmen make good eating!" He rubbed his stomach, grinned at her.

"I'm too thin," she said, in what she hoped was a jocular tone. "You'll have to fatten me up first."

She noticed that cowardice, either in a captive or traveler, elicited from Indians far more savage treatment than a staunch, resolute attitude.

The Indians gave a shout of approval, she was ordered to cut a notch in their stone calendar and put her hand on the head of the new chief. She never was completely sure whether they meant to carry out their threats or if the threats were a sign of humor. The Indian was like a child, acting on impulse, changing his mind in a second. She had to trust they feared the wrath of Colonel Tupper, should he return to find Robert Shurtliff missing.

She was invited to join the coronation ceremonies for the new chief. To the tune of tom-toms she ate with the Indians instead of being eaten.

Early the next morning she noticed a large group equipping themselves for a hunting trip. She thought she should do her part in providing food since she was consuming it, and happily offered to go along. The Indians cheered as though she were a chivalrous knight entering the lists of competition at a Christian King's tournament.

Before setting off, Deborah's musket was exchanged for a hunting rifle and tomahawk. Some of the Indians took only bows and arrows as there were not enough guns to go around. Deborah was challenged to fire twenty rods at a target to prove her marksmanship. The Indians with guns defeated her by a small margin, except for one old Indian who seemed dim-sighted and cast her a look of hatred, as though he could devour her on the spot without even bothering to boil her.

Their route took them down the Ohio, which they crossed frequently in canoes as they made their way through one vast unbroken wilderness. The second day out Deborah spied a wild turkey high on a tree, took aim, shot it down just as the old Indian was preparing to shoot. The rest of the Indians, including a twelve-year-old boy, danced around her, praising her as a quick and true marksman. But she saw only envy and malice flame in the eyes of the old man, humiliated before his fellow tribesman by a lone soldier.

They encamped that night near the Muskingum River under an

ancient hickory tree with a chasm cut through its trunk wide enough for two men to walk abreast. At sunrise they divided into two parties. The jealous Indian, the boy and Deborah made up one party—by chance or perhaps design, she thought.

The old Indian led the way, like a buck bounding from cliff to valley. As they ascended a hill, the hunting dogs startled a buffalo. Deborah had competed with boys all her life to try to win the love of her mother; competition was second nature to her. In silent rivalry with the old Indian for the second time in as many days, she shot the buffalo just as the old man was bringing his piece to an aim. The boy looked at her again in admiration but the older man stared at Deborah as if he wanted to aim the piece at her head. Perhaps in reparation, or because she was afraid of the hatred she read in his eyes, she allowed him to carve and roast pieces of the buffalo meat for a tasty meal, hanging the skin, which would be taken with them on their return to dry. The rest of the day's hunt yielded three more wild turkeys.

The trio took a canoe for a rapid voyage down the Muskingum. She saw many waterfowl as the boy told her the Indians had no use for them and therefore would not shoot them. Indians do not kill game wantonly, she thought, wishing the same could be said of many white men who called themselves civilized but at whose approach beasts, birds and fishes fled.

The next morning they crossed the Ohio again. That night, as tired as she felt, Deborah could not sleep: her sixth sense warned her to be on guard. Hour after hour the note of the owl and the howl of the wolf kept her company. She noticed the old Indian was restless, frequently half rising as though to make sure the fire was not out but casting a furtive eye in her direction each time.

Feigning sleep, she suddenly opened her eyes to see him soundlessly crawling towards her, like a cat ready to pounce on its prey.

As he drew near, she glimpsed a tomahawk in his hand. He obviously was preparing to bury it in her skull.

When he came within two yards, she sprang up, seized the hunting gun and shot him through the chest. The Indian fell dead at her feet. Reluctant as she was to shoot a human being, Deborah also felt a surge of satisfaction in killing off this enemy. She was taking revenge on all men, past and present, who had violated her or her country's integrity.

The explosion of the gun woke the boy. On seeing the dead Indian he screamed in terror, then tore at the ground like a young, mad bull, fearing she would kill him next.

She walked over to the boy, took his hand, led him to the body and showed him the tomahawk locked stiffly in the old man's fingers. "He was going to kill me. I had to save myself," she softly explained. "I won't hurt you if you'll promise on your life not to tell anyone." If the other Indians found out what she had done, even though she had killed in self defense they probably would burn her at the stake in revenge.

"I promise," he said.

She trusted him to keep quiet about the killing, bank on his understanding she would have been murdered if she had not fired first. But to make sure, she asked him to call on "the great Spirit who sees all things" as witness to his promise, with punishment in store if he dared break it.

When morning came they carried the old Indian's body to the river, strapped it to a heavy stone, then sank it. They walked miles up and down hills, through thick forests without seeing one sign of human life. At night, cold, starved and fatigued, they lit a fire. It attracted the howlings of wild animals the boy said were bears and foxes. Deborah quickly agreed to put out the fire.

The boy was so frightened that he finally ran up a tree like a squirrel. She followed, climbing more slowly. At first they dared not sleep for fear of falling out of the tree. After many vain attempts at securing herself, Deborah tied herself to a limb with the strap of her musket and her handkerchief. She slept fitfully until daybreak, woke to find rain streaming down her face. She called out to the boy above but he did not answer. He was busily disengaging his long black hair from the branches around which he had entwined it to keep from falling to the ground.

After climbing down and stretching out the kinks in their bodies from the awkward sleeping positions, they walked eastward. Traveling all day without food except a few wild grapes left them tired, hungry and exhausted. Searching for a settlement or Indian tribe, they reached a mountainous precipice late that afternoon. Wearily they trudged the four miles around its base, finally discovered a path leading upward. After a quarter of a mile climb they came upon a small waterfall, drank deeply of its cool waters, spent the night beside it.

In the morning, still exhausted, they had to decide whether to retreat or try to reach the summit. Deborah felt wedged between the Scylla of scaling the huge mountainside and the Charybdis of descending its steep slope. The boy started to weep bitterly, the first tears Deborah had seen an Indian shed. She thought, People are much the same no matter what their origin, by and large we are all simply human beings.

"Let's go on up," she said. "We'll get a good view and might see some way of escape."

After a strenuous climb past sharp ledges and rocky crevices they reached a grassy knoll. Deborah threw herself on the ground for a moment's rest. As she later revealed to Mann, she thought how undignified it would be to die in this alien spot, relatives and friends unaware she had perished somewhere in the new frontier. Tears filled her eyes at memories of Middleborough, dew dancing on the grass at dawn, the aphrodisiac fragrance of newly-mown hay, as she realized she might never see New England again. With these thoughts Deborah dozed off in the heat of the sun.

She was awakened by the report of a gun. Deborah jumped to her feet to find both her musket and the boy had vanished. She walked up the precipice in the direction of the shot, saw the Indian youth standing quietly, holding her gun.

He handed it to her, said, "I shot it so you would come. When you didn't follow me I thought you might have hurt yourself or died."

"I fell asleep," she said.

She wondered why he had taken her musket and left without her. She thought perhaps he had planned to abandon her, then changed his mind. Or perhaps he felt so humiliated about her seeing him in tears that he could not bear to face her. She decided not to ask. She probably would not have believed his response anyway.

He gave her a handful of grapes, said, "Follow me." Regaining his pride, he led the way to an immense rock, crept inside through a fissure. In front of them spread a feast of groundnuts, wild beans, hops and gourds. They ate hungrily, filling up for the first time in days.

Feeling new energy Deborah saw at a distance a large body of water framed by the stately mountains. At that moment they heard the firing of guns from far below. Deborah raised her musket in an answering shot. Her fire was returned. They had found rescuers.

Deborah and the boy discovered hidden reserves that enabled them to race down the precipice. At its base they faced thirty Indians sitting by a brook in front of which large piles of isinglass stood as silent sentinels. She heard one Indian say, "Detroit," pointing to bright red and orange blankets. She surmised the tribes had visited that post to obtain provisions and blankets.

The boy explained he and the young soldier were lost. He

described the location of his camping grounds. Knowing Indians of this area had been taking part in the Revolution on both sides, depending on whichever bribed them more, Deborah announced peace had just been declared. The Indians took this matter-of-factly, they were far more interested in peace between the red and white man.

To her amazement, Deborah noticed one member of the group was not an Indian but a white girl. She walked over to the girl, who had a pale, grief-worn face, asked, "What are you doing here?"

The young woman told her the Indians had kidnapped her, seizing her out of the arms of her mother and father the year before. She said she had already been sold several times to different tribes. She started to cry, saying, "They're going to burn me at the stake."

"Why?" Deborah asked.

"Because I let a papoose fall one day when I was carrying a very heavy load."

"Did it die?" Deborah asked.

"No, but it was sick for weeks," the girl said. "They decided I had to be punished."

"I'll try to find some way to save you," Deborah promised.

"How?" the girl wailed.

"I don't know yet but I'll think of something," Deborah said.

With the Indians guiding them, they found the boy's tribe in a day. As her welcome, the new chief said to Deborah accusingly, "You run away to look for the Colonel. You frightened."

Grateful to Deborah, the boy defended her. He told the chief, "She save my life when the old Indian die. She stay with me so we both get back." He kept his word that he would never mention the way in which the old Indian had died after trying to kill Deborah. The chief apologized to Deborah, thanked her for bringing the boy home.

Deborah said to the chief, suddenly thinking of a way to save the girl, "Will you give me a squaw as bride in return for saving the boy's life? I will pay you a high ransom. Two guns." She knew the Indians were greedy for guns.

"No squaw marry white man," the chief said emphatically, as Deborah knew he would.

"What about the white girl?" she asked. "You give an Indian one gun and you keep the other."

"You take the white girl for three guns," said the chief. "I keep two."

"All right." Deborah admired his skill as trader. "You'll get the guns when Colonel Tupper comes back." She spoke as one expert to another, proving she was not above a bit of manipulation herself when lives were at stake.

That night the girl and Deborah were ordered to share the same bearskin, following the marriage rites of the Indians. The girl lay down next to Deborah gingerly, then swiftly sat up in fear, looking as though she were about to be tortured.

"What's the matter?" Deborah asked.

"I'm a virgin," the girl whispered. "In spite of their cruelty, the Indians never physically touched me. They were ashamed of me."

"Don't worry," Deborah reassured her. "I won't insist on any marital rights until we are united by a minister." She did not want the girl to know of her disguise, even though it would have lessened her fear.

The girl looked at Deborah gratefully, then curled up on her side of the bearskin, fell asleep. Deborah felt relieved and slightly amused at putting one over on the Indians.

The next day Colonel Tupper and his expedition arrived at the camp, his diggings completed. Deborah had never felt so happy to see a familiar face. She did not trust the Indians to keep their word, any minute they might turn on her, even kill her, as the old Indian had tried to do.

She told Colonel Tupper the Indians were asking a ransom of

three guns to free the white girl. He consented to give them the guns.

The expedition decided to return to Philadelphia at once. The trip back held no storms, the way was continuously clear. In Philadelphia Colonel Tupper bought the girl a new dress, gave her money to travel to her parents' home in James City, Virginia. Deborah never revealed her masquerade, allowed the girl to think the noble Robert Shurtliff had devised the idea of a false marriage to free her from captivity. Out of her gratitude, the girl kissed Deborah goodbye on the cheek.

As a result of Deborah's journey to the Shenandoah and Ohio rivers, she decided she had enough of Indians to last the rest of her life. She felt even greater admiration for her ancestors who had lived out their days and nights under the continuous threat of Indian attack.

Now she had to carry through on her promise to see Dr. Binney before she left Philadelphia for West Point, where, no doubt, everyone believed her dead from the malignant flu that had killed so many American soldiers.

THE SEALED
LETTER

Deborah felt deeply grateful to
Dr. Binney, not only for the chance to see the grandeur of the new
territory to the west but for safeguarding her secret. Keeping her
promise to visit him before heading north, she went directly to his
home the minute she returned to Philadelphia.

It was a Saturday and he and his wife warmly welcomed her,
then served luncheon. Afterwards Dr. Binney invited Deborah to
his library where they had their previous talk.

She thanked him for arranging the fascinating trip, told him she
had seen wild, beautiful country, luxurious beyond belief with

monumental trees and bushes. She then informed him she was returning at once to her regiment at West Point.

"Are you going to tell them the truth?" he asked quietly.

"As much as I can." She ignored the deeper implications of his question.

He was thoughtful for a moment, then offered, "Since you have no money, I will pay your passage to West Point."

Moved by the kindness of this fatherly stranger, she said, "I can't let you do that, I owe you too much already. But I will take a loan."

"Please accept it as a gift," he insisted. "And I suggest you rest here at least twenty-four hours before you leave on that long trip."

"Thank you." She struggled to hold back tears. She could never repay this generous, understanding man who had saved her life, taken her into his home, asked his wife to nurse her to health and who, as far as she knew, had not revealed her secret to anyone but the matron of the hospital. Someday she would write him openly about her feelings of gratitude.

But there was someone she felt she had to write to immediately. She had an important matter to clear up. It troubled her she had caused pain to Dr. Binney's niece. Deborah felt in all fairness that for the first time she had to reveal her true identity. The young woman deserved the truth.

With trepidation she asked Mrs. Binney for her niece's address in Baltimore. She wrote the young woman at once, begged her forgiveness, saying she wanted to spare her hurt and would never forget her many kindnesses. She signed the note Robert Shurtliff, added the words, "One of your own sex." She trusted the niece to figure out the truth.

Dr. Binney reserved Deborah a seat on the stagecoach that would take her to Elizabeth Town, a village in New Jersey fourteen miles southwest of New York City. From there she would board a stage boat for the rest of the trip up the Hudson River to West Point. The British still occupied New York but would not fire on anyone since hostilities had ceased.

As Deborah was ready to leave the house, Dr. Binney took her aside. He said with compassion, "May I give a short prescription as a token of my regard? Be careful of your health and continue to be as discreet in everything as you have been true to the cause of freedom."

He added, "Someday your country will place a wreath of undying fame on your brow."

Deborah's eyes misted over with tears, Dr. Binney pretended he did not see them. He handed her a sealed letter, addressed to General Paterson.

"Please don't fail to deliver this," he said. "It contains a tribute to you—and to the general."

Dr. Binney and his wife escorted Deborah to the depot in horse and carriage. She felt forlorn leaving this kindly couple. She had finally found a caring father figure and now she had to leave him forever. Father, grandfather, grandmother, brothers, Preacher Taylor—it was the same sad story of those she had lost, who were important in her life, people she had loved.

She felt a sudden impulse to kiss the doctor goodbye but forced herself to check it. An action appropriate for Deborah Sampson would hardly be fit for Robert Shurtliff, the soldier.

She and twelve other passengers riding the stagecoach reached Elizabeth Town on October 12, 1783, a cold gray day. The town was situated on the Arthur Kill, which flowed into the lower part of Newark Bay, then Kill Van Kull and upper New York Bay.

When they arrived, Deborah discovered to her dismay that the stage boat had already sailed. Eager to continue their journey at once, she and her fellow passengers found a skiff and a skipper to navigate it. He complained of rainy weather and a strong wind that had started to blow like an equinoctial gale, but persuaded by the anxious passengers, and perhaps loath to lose an extra day's pay, he agreed to get under way in the gale. It was a decision all were to regret.

As they approached lower Newark Bay, the passengers saw a shallop with nineteen passengers on board caught in the fury of a violent wind. With pounding hearts they helplessly watched it founder in the deep channel, then sink. All nineteen passengers were drowned. Deborah heard their screams as the angry waves rolled over them, devoured them one by one like greedy monsters of the deep. The sight of this tragedy made her feel as if she had been present at her father's drowning. She would picture this scene over and over as long as she lived.

One of Deborah's shipmates, seeing the shadow of Staten Island's hills in the distance, anxiously asked the skipper as he struggled to maintain control of the wheel, "Could we swim there if this boat sinks?"

Reluctantly the skipper told him he did not think anyone wearing heavy clothes could make shore in the storm.

A few moments later the skipper lost complete control of the skiff as the rapid current and roaring wind tossed it about like a feather. Water started to pour in over the sides. The passengers scurried around panic-stricken, seeking the safest possible spot for themselves and their loved ones as the water rose higher and higher.

Suddenly a towering wave swamped the entire ship, within moments it started to sink. They all feared they would share the fate of the nineteen shallop passengers they had watched drown just moments before. Deborah struggled to remain upright as the surging water and blasting winds propelled her down the shifting slopes of the ship.

She managed until the end to hold above water her small trunk.

It contained the three shirts Dr. Binney's niece had given her, extra socks and the diary she faithfully kept day by day, except when ill. Finally she realized there was no hope of saving the trunk. She would be lucky to escape with her life. She was thankful she had learned to swim after the Croton River episode.

She fought the rising water as she placed a Moroccan purse containing the sealed letter from Dr. Binney in her haversack. She then flung it over her left shoulder, valiantly leaped into the sea.

Swimming toward the Staten Island shore against the mammoth waves and fierce currents, she soon became numb from the cold and fatigue. Still, she continued swimming like an automaton. She felt wearier by the moment as the distance stretched interminably before her. No matter how far she swam, the land appeared the same distance away.

Finally she thought she could swim no further, she was ready to give up the fight. She said to herself, *I'm sorry I'll never see my mother again but it won't be so hard to die. I've accomplished what was most important to me.* She had the fleeting thought, *I'll be with my father at the bottom of the sea, if that is where he lies.*

But when Deborah put down her feet to touch what she thought would be eternity, she contacted instead soft, springy sand. Her ordeal was not yet over, giant breakers pummelled her from beneath. She coughed, spit up water, gasped for every breath. Finally she reached out to a bed of rushes, managed to hold onto them until she could breathe normally.

She tried twice to reach shore but giant waves snatched her back to sea. On the third attempt she stepped on a sand bank, found the bottom gloriously hard. Summoning up what little strength remained, she bent into the fury of the wind, managed to walk slowly to the shore. There she collapsed on the beach, unable to move a single step further. Others who also reached the shore lay stretched out nearby.

Deborah spent the night lying on the sand, too weary to move, thankful for the feel of earth beneath her. By morning the wind had died down and the skipper, who survived, took stock. Deborah was surprised to find that all but two passengers, who had gone down with the skiff, had mastered the disastrous journey.

They were rescued by a special boat sent to cruise for survivors, taken back to Elizabeth Town where they were fed and their clothes dried. Then they were put on a stage boat and in calm weather set out again for West Point.

The boat sailed past the New York skyline, where two- and three-story buildings clustered around the bay and the East River. Deborah could almost reach out and touch the British ships of war, placid at the docks, some taking on supplies, not for a new campaign on America's blood-drenched shores but to recross the Atlantic for home. She felt intense hatred for the redcoats, then sudden sorrow for the waste of it all—the bloodshed, the deaths, the maimings, the barbaric, senseless act that was war.

The Treaty of Paris finally had been ratified in Europe on September 3, the same day she had saved herself from being scalped by the savage old Indian for daring to be a better marksman than he. The British now planned to evacuate New York as soon as all ships were ready.

As Deborah sailed up the Hudson she saw Tarrytown, glimpsed in the distance the hills where she had been wounded by the two Tory musket balls. She noted where the perfidious Widow Hunt had tried to arrange the slaughter of the patriot scouting party. All warfare now lay behind her, she was no longer in danger, about to be discharged from the army.

Deborah realized she felt very nervous about the contents of Dr. Binney's letter to General Patterson, still ensconced in her haversack. She suspected what it would say. From Dr. Binney's words— "It contains a tribute to you—and to the general"—she could only conclude that with the war nearly over, Dr. Binney felt compelled to tell General Paterson the truth.

She had wanted somehow to lose the letter. It would have been easy enough to get rid of it when the skiff sank beneath her. She only had to let the haversack float away in the fury of the wind to retain her secret forever.

But her promise to Dr. Binney, a man for whom she felt deep affection and gratitude, was stronger than her wish to destroy the letter. In the end her conscience proved stronger than the need to protect herself.

"DOES THAT UNIFORM CONCEAL A WOMAN'S FORM?"

A number of familiar faces in Deborah's company were missing. Congress, expecting final peace terms, had ordered furloughs for some of the men to start in June. After the definitive treaty of peace was ratified on September 23, Congress issued a proclamation disbanding the army as of November 3. Many of the soldiers left before her return to West Point.

The men she knew welcomed her warmly. As she suspected, they thought she had died of the malignant fever. Several had seen her carried off unconscious to the hospital, believed she would never return. She was moved now by their concern but wondered if they would care about her if they knew she was a woman.

The day General Washington received word by courier of the ratification of the final treaty, he appeared at noon before the troops in New Windsor to announce peace. The war-weary soldiers let out three "Huzzahs!" Chaplain John Ganno offered a prayer, followed by singing and instrumental music, then an extra ration of rum for each man. The troops drank to peace and independence. The West Point garrison also received extra rations of rum—there might be shortages of food, but never rum.

Deborah was surprised to find she had mixed feelings about the disbanding of the army. Thrilled by the cessation of hostilities and needless deaths of thousands of young men, and yearning to return to the peace and dignity of home, she also felt saddened at the thought of ending her army career.

The year-and-a-half of service had been the most exciting time of her otherwise unexciting life. She had traveled far, enjoyed adventures open to few men, let alone women, of the times. She had lived out her dream, a pleasure given few humans. Close to death several times because of malignant fever, gun-shot wounds, Indian tomahawks and near-drowning, Deborah thanked God she had lived long enough to accomplish her life's missions.

But, terrified of the consequences, she did not want to be unmasked. Yet, whatever her fate, she knew she would leave the army feeling proud of and fulfilled by the part she played in serving her country. She would miss the excitement, the comradery, the days of being a heroine like her grandmother's two idols. She accepted that it had to end soon, just as she understood she would have to confront General Paterson with Dr. Binney's letter.

Dreading the moment, Deborah delayed her request to call on General Paterson several times. One moment she felt guilty of a debased act, as if she had committed adultery or given birth to an illegitimate child. The next moment she felt proud—her only crime after all had been to fight for the honor of her country.

Finally, toward the end of November 1783, she no longer dared postpone her most dangerous mission. She slowly walked to General Paterson's quarters, forced herself to ask Major Haskell if she could see the general. She explained she had an important letter to deliver from Dr. Barnabus Binney of Philadelphia.

Major Haskell showed her into General Paterson's office. The General stood up as she entered, shook her hand warmly, said with a smile, "Welcome back, Private Shurtliff. We were informed you had died of the fever. My wife and I felt very sad at the thought of never seeing you again."

She wasted no words, quickly handed him the sealed letter, thinking, as she later told Mann, "a palsied man or an aspen leaf never shook more than my hand." To General Paterson she said only, "Dr. Binney of Philadelphia asked me to give you this, sir."

"Fine surgeon. Fine man," said General Paterson. "I met him at the battle of Bunker Hill. How is he?"

"In the best of health when I saw him about two weeks ago, sir," Deborah answered.

The general thanked her for bringing the letter, told her once again how delighted he was to see her alive and well.

Taking this as dismissal, she saluted and walked out of his office. She did not wish to be present when he read the letter, fearing the bombshell that lay in it.

She sat on her bunk trembling in fear, awaiting the inevitable— a messenger from General Paterson. He arrived within the half hour, asked her to accompany him to the general's quarters.

As she marched back, Deborah thought of an Indian prayer she had heard on her visit west: "Spirits of the brave, lend me fortitude." She was sure that before long she would face a firing squad, the modern equivalent of her heroine, Joan of Arc, burning at the stake.

As she entered the general's office for the second time that day she saw General Paterson, who had always treated her with respect, chosen her above all other soldiers to be his aide-de-camp when Major Haskell fell ill, staring at her as though he could not believe his eyes.

He asked her to sit down, as he then did. Choosing his words carefully, he said, "Private Robert Shurtliff, you have been in my brigade a year-and-a-half. You have always been brave, vigilant and faithful. You have a more distinguished record than most of your fellow soldiers."

The General seemed to be fighting to control many opposing emotions. He coughed several times, then went on in a pleading tone, "Now I must ask you a vital question."

He stopped, drew in his breath, let it out, then asked, "Does that uniform conceal a woman's form?"

Deborah felt not like a veteran of battle but as weak and effeminate as a powerless woman, as insignificant as the child exposed and humiliated by her Uncle Simeon when she was four-and-a-half years old. Why could she not give herself up to justice as courageously as she had fought the enemy, instead of feeling she would welcome a phial of volatile salts?

She thought she saw a glint of tears in the general's eyes, as though he were deeply moved by the idea that any woman could have endured the hardships and dangers of army life during war. The contrast between the general's tears and her own fear of being shot for her "crime" apparently proved too overwhelming for Deborah to contemplate.

But if it were true that the general was sympathetic, not punitive, she would not have to fear for her life. It was too much to take in all at once. She stood up, felt faint, grabbed a chair to steady herself.

She still had not answered the general's question, she knew her silence held the answer. Her uniform spoke for her.

"Please, sir, don't have me shot," she begged. "I only wanted to fight for my country."

Her confession made her feel faint again and she started to slip to the floor. General Paterson raced to her side, gently lifted her up, placed her back in the chair. As he returned to his desk he said, "You are a very courageous woman, as Dr. Binney wrote. He told me how he discovered you were a woman as you lay near death in his hospital. He pointed out the uniqueness of your situation and asked me to treat you as a heroine."

He stared closely at her face, then asked in wonder, "Can it really be so?"

Deborah saw in the compassion within his eyes that the general would not willingly harm her. She now felt ready to brave the truth and its consequences.

"It's true, sir," she said courageously. "My name is Deborah Sampson. I live in Middleborough, Massachusetts. I was born in Plympton. Some of my ancestors came over on the *Mayflower*."

Terror returning, she quickly asked, "Will you spare my life?"

"You are not only completely safe from harm but entitled to full respect," he said. "I'm going to take care of your discharge at once. I'll see you have safe passage back to your family."

Then he muttered as though to himself, "I still cannot believe it."

"I'll prove it, sir," she said, in a burst of self-confidence, born of his sanction of her daring deed, "if you'll lend me one of your wife's dresses and allow me a few minutes to change."

Her eyes lit up in anticipation of wearing female garments after a year and a half in men's clothing. The general, noting the happiness on her face, said, "Wait here."

He left the office, soon returned carrying one of his wife's dresses. He handed it to Deborah, saying, "You can change in your old room upstairs. When you're ready, come back here."

She reached out for the dress, ran up the steps to the bedroom she occupied when Major Haskell fell ill. She stepped out of the army uniform, lowered the linen strip she had replaced during her days recuperating at Dr. Binney's house. She recalled with nostalgia the first time she had bound her breasts, slipped off her female clothing. It seemed a lifetime ago.

She tried on the dark blue, ankle-length dress. It felt strange to wear feminine finery but she was also filled with a swelling sense of pleasure. She completed the womanly picture by borrowing a pair of shoes and rouge for her cheeks from Mrs. Paterson's room. She had accomplished her deepest mission in life. Now she could be a woman once more.

As she entered General Paterson's office she saw him stare at her once again as though he could not believe his eyes. But this time, she thought, with as much ecstasy on the face of a man as she had ever seen or was likely to see. He seemed enraptured by her transformation, as though witnessing a miracle. With her newly restored femininity, Deborah could not help feeling delighted too. If this revered general could accept that she was a woman, then she also should be able to accept it.

"This is truly theatrical!" he told her. "I must send for Colonel Jackson and see if he recognizes you."

Five minutes later Colonel Jackson, who had taken over as head of her regiment a few weeks after she had first arrived at West Point, who had granted her request to attack the Van Tassel mansion, who had praised her courage under fire, walked into the room.

He saluted the general, then turned to Deborah and asked, "Who do I have the pleasure of addressing?"

General Paterson answered, "This is Miss Deborah Sampson. She is from your own state, the cradle of liberty—and a fit person she is to rock it, till the infant is full grown."

"I'm happy to meet you, Miss Sampson," Colonel Jackson said.

"You have met her many times," General Paterson pointed out.

"I'm afraid you're in error, General," Colonel Jackson answered. "I have never met this soft-spoken, attractive lady. I would have recalled it because of her charm."

General Paterson then casually asked, as though to change the subject, "Have you received any information about Private Robert Shurtliff?"

"No word for months," the Colonel said. "That brave fellow's dead of the fever in Philadelphia."

"Our revolution is full of miracles," said the general. He turned to Deborah, "This young lady exceeds them all."

Then he ordered Colonel Jackson, "Examine her closely. She was taught by your own example in the army. See if you do not recognize Robert Shurtliff."

Colonel Jackson whirled to look at her. He paled as he peered closely into her eyes. He muttered, "It can't be."

"But it is," said General Paterson. "Meet Robert Shurtliff."

"The miracle of miracles," said a dazed Colonel Jackson.

He stood up, wiped his brow with his handkerchief, announced, "I need time to recover," and fled.

"He's taking it hard," the general told Deborah. "But that's understandable. So did I at first. You are a unique young lady, Miss Sampson."

Then he said, his voice showing concern, "Until you leave, I will assign you a room of your own in my quarters."

"Thank you, sir." This kindly man possessed more understanding than she ever dreamed a man in his position would show.

"Please keep on the dress," he said. "My wife will be happy to give it to you as a gift."

Conflicting thoughts ran through Deborah's head. She enjoyed wearing feminine clothes again, would have liked to accept the gift of a dress from the generous general. But she had worn the uniform proudly for a year-and-a-half, had fought long and hard for such a privilege. She was still officially in the army.

"Thank you, sir," she responded, "but I prefer wearing my uniform, if you don't mind."

"As you wish," the General said. "But expect a lot of teasing. News of this sort will quickly fly through the air."

"I can handle it, sir," she said. "No one ever suspected I was a woman. They treated me no differently than they did each other."

"No . . . er . . . flirtations?" He sounded surprised.

"Not a one, sir." She drew herself erect. "I enlisted to fight for my country. Not to seduce soldiers."

"I believe you, Miss Sampson." His voice was earnest.

Then he asked, "Do your mother and father know about this?"

"We believe my father's been dead for eighteen years, sir," she said, added wistfully, "at least we believed at first he drowned at sea when his ship went down. Later there were rumors he was living in Maine with a wife and young children but we did not try to find out if this was true."

Of her mother she said, "I never told her about entering the army because she would have stopped me."

General Patterson seemed once again lost in thought. Then he said, "I remember a man who came here about a year ago asking for a Deborah Sampson. He thought she might have joined the army dressed as a man. We all just laughed at this idea."

"I recognized him, sir," she admitted. "My mother wanted me to marry him because he was fairly rich and respectable. But I wasn't in love with him."

"And he didn't recognize you?" The general seemed amazed.

"No, sir. We passed each other just outside the barracks. I kept my eyes averted. He went on his way."

"Unbelievable!" the General exclaimed. Then he added, "Will you do one thing for me, Miss Sampson?"

"Anything, sir." She would walk on broken glass in bare feet all the way south to the Potomac if the general requested it. "You have spared my life and I shall be eternally grateful."

"Will you walk around the grounds as you are now dressed and see if anyone recognizes you?" he asked. "I will accompany you."

She felt excited at the idea of a test walk, as curious as the general to learn the results. By his side she strode through the tented grounds to see if any of the officers and soldiers recognized her. There were men who had marched with her over the frozen trails of the Adirondacks, swum with her across the icy Croton River as they fled death from the Tories, carried her with two musket balls in her thigh to the French hospital at Crompound. Not one gave a sign they knew who she was.

Again Deborah felt conflicting emotions. While aglow at the success of her ruse, she also felt moments of disappointment that no one man had seen the real Deborah beneath her disguise. She wanted to shout, "Boys, comrades-in-arms, it's me, Robert. Doesn't anyone really look at me? I am the same person in uniform or out, whether you call me Deborah or Robert."

"You serve well as either man or woman," General Paterson said as they returned to his office.

She replied, "Thank you, sir," and left for his wife's bedroom, where she stepped out of Mrs. Paterson's dress and once again into the garb and role of Robert Shurtliff.

When she returned to the barracks she experienced a proud moment she would never forget. By now the news had spread throughout the fortress and she was greeted with cheers and hurrahs by her compatriots. Soldiers crowded around her, with amazement, surprise and amusement on their faces.

Most congratulated her, a few asked, "Why did you do it?" Others were eager to know, "How were you able to keep it from us?"

Several admitted, "If you weren't here to prove it this very moment, we'd never believe it."

A few roughnecks demanded she show positive proof she was a woman. She ignored their insults.

Deborah received an honorable discharge on October 25, 1783, signed by General Henry Knox, commandant of West Point. Testimonials of her faithful performances and exemplary conduct were signed by General Paterson as head of the First Brigade, General Shepard, originally head of the Fourth Massachusetts Regiment, and his successor Colonel Jackson.

The discovery she was a woman had come at a propitious moment. The army was eager to send its men home. An auction had disposed of the buildings at the New Windsor cantonment, some of which Deborah had helped erect. Few traces of the huts remained as the land once again was used for farming. West Point and Fort Pitt, Pennsylvania, were designated as the main depositories of military stores.

A small force would be retained at West Point for garrison duty. Together with what disbanded men and militia could be assembled, they were to march to New York in December to take possession of that city on its evacuation by the British. If Deborah had not been exposed as a woman, she might have been one of the soldiers to march with General Washington and Governor Clinton into New York. She would have enjoyed both that honor and the chance to explore New York, the only one of the large cities she had not viewed almost block-by-block.

She saw officers and private soldiers leave West Point, embracing each other as they parted, heading for far corners of the colonies, but forever bound by the common dangers and suffering they had endured together. She yearned to embrace the others as well, but as a woman exposed she had to be satisfied with more formal good-byes.

Someday, she thought, as she later told Mann, men and women will be free from the restrictions of gender, allowed to express warm feelings regardless of their sex.

Then it was her turn to leave. General Paterson and Colonel Jackson walked her down to the dock. She was scheduled to sail on a sloop of war to New York—she would indeed see the city before she left for home. From there she would board Captain Allen's packet for Providence, her trip paid for by the army—the only money she would ever receive for her year-and-a-half of service.

Both General Paterson and Colonel Jackson shook her hand as she stood beside them, still wearing her uniform. The general said, "God be with you and protect you, Miss Sampson."

Deborah fought back tears on leaving these two compassionate men, inundated by memories of her father disappearing into the distance forever, nineteen years ago.

As the sloop slipped away from the cliffs, Deborah looked up at the plateau where she had spent many an arduous but gratifying hour. She had enlisted for three years but served only half that time. It had been a fascinating, exciting, although often dangerous eighteen months. She would cherish every memory of it the rest of her life.

The army had let her live in spite of her duplicity. That was more than she had expected. Now she would have to face returning home where, she realized, the men and women might not be so understanding.

12

❧

DEBORAH'S VITAL DREAM

On the packet boat homeward Deborah had a recurring dream that portrayed the major conflicts of her life—the hidden purpose of a dream. This was the last time it would occur.

Up to now she could never forget a terrifying nightmare that every so often disturbed her sleep. The dream appeared the first time when she was fifteen, on April 15, 1775, four days before the battle of Lexington, about forty miles from where she lived.

Most dreams stem from our two strongest feelings—love and hate—often combining the two. These disparate emotions appeared openly in Deborah's poignant dream, revealing the reasons she was driven to enlist in the Continental Army.

The dream started pleasurably—the feeling of love appeared first. Deborah saw herself running happily through fields and groves where deer grazed and birds caroled. She raced to the top of a hill, the better to survey the natural beauty below. She sat down to rest at the summit.

Suddenly the serene azure sky became veiled in blackness. Lightning flashed, loud peals of thunder filled the air, no longer fragrant with flowers but smelling of the stench of sulphur. The peaceful valley changed to a roaring sea in which high waves dashed ships against rocks, smashing them to splinters (her picture of how her father died).

Out of the boiling waves rose a hideous serpent writhing its way toward her, leaving a trail of blood. She ran to her home, the serpent in pursuit. When she reached her room, expecting to be safe, she threw open the door only to find the serpent coiled inside, its body spreading almost to the four walls. It flicked its tongue wildly at her, its eyes balls of fire. She tried to scream for help but no sound emerged from her terrified mouth.

A voice ordered, "Arise, stand on your feet, gird yourself and prepare to encounter your enemy." She looked around the room but could find no weapon for her defense. She jumped on her bed, the serpent slithered after her as though to swallow her whole. Suddenly she saw a bludgeon, a short club with a thick, heavy end. She picked it up, attacked the serpent.

It turned and moved toward the door as she pursued it, lowering its head and trying to strike her with its tail. It then turned into a fish, divided into several sections, decorated with large letters of yellow gilt, forming the words, "The rights of man are at our disposal." (Deborah was trying to assure herself she was entitled to the same rights a man possessed.)

The fish fled into the street as Deborah followed, caught up with it. She kept flailing away until she dislocated every joint. It lay in pieces on the ground.

But suddenly the pieces reunited in the shape of a giant bull. It rushed at her with a roar, trying to gore her with its horns. She struck it in such fury with the bludgeon that the ground trembled as it fell. The bull too dissolved into pieces. When she ran to gather them up, she found only a pool of jelly.

Each time she woke from the nightmare, just as she reached the pool of jelly, she screamed. The thought of finding nothing where there had been something terrified her. She felt like a murderer even though she had acted to save her very life.

When Deborah was five-and-a-half years old her father had been reported shipwrecked and drowned in a turbulent storm, like the one in her dream. But later rumors arose suggesting he had never been lost at sea but returned to live in Maine where he married another woman, possibly two. It would be natural for her to feel deep anger at her deserting father. In revenge she attacked him, pictured in the dream as a monstrous serpent who loathed her, hacking him to pieces. When he turned into a bull, she also destroyed this version of him.

In the Continental Army she acted out her anger as she fired guns at Tories and redcoats, the serpents and bulls of her real life. Never did a hunter in pursuit of game feel more zealous than Deborah in search of the enemy. She believed Tories the true villains, traitors all to those who wished to live in loving peace, as she had wished to live with her father.

She could feel the deep hatred in her heart each time she physically wounded an enemy soldier. Part of her had entered the army to free the colonies from the cruel British, but part of her had joined out of a wish to kill the man who had forsaken her so early in her life. In her fantasy, the British villain and her father were one and the same.

Where did Deborah find the strength to defy family, society and the government, then seek the forbidden career she craved? The answer lies encoded in her dramatic nightmare. It reflects both the confidence and love she felt in a happy childhood before the age of five and the hatred that encompassed her mind after her beloved father left his family.

The grown-up Deborah was driven consciously and, far more so, unconsciously to free herself from the devastating trauma of the loss of her father. She threw off what could have been a strangling neurosis so she could resume the natural emotional development interrupted by her father's desertion and assumed death. First this had to be acted out on the battlefield before she could accept her female destiny, find the husband and children she desired.

Joining the revolutionary army allowed Deborah to express her deeply buried rage—a form of expression permitted only to men at that time in American history. She felt relief as she could fight and vanquish a man. Content with this acting out of her wrath, she could then face her feelings as a woman.

Her nightmare starts out pleasurably, as did her early life, living with both a mother and father. The fact that she races to the top of the hill paints a picture of an idyllic early childhood in which she easily reached the pinnacle of normal development. Her mother was a gentle woman with whom Deborah could identify, as symbolized by the deer who grazed contently. Deborah's small siblings were depicted as happy, caroling birds.

Deborah later assured her mother that she loved her in spite of her early anger at being farmed out to strangers. Except for the year and a half of army service, Deborah kept in touch with her mother throughout her life.

But the fact Deborah had been ousted from home when her father had supposedly died and her mother could no longer take care of her older children certainly contributed to her ambivalent feelings toward her mother. Deborah was unjust when she withheld from her mother the fact she had joined the army.

When she later told her mother she did not have the courage to report her enlistment, her mother replied, "But that wasn't fair." Deborah agreed, which suggests she should have known her mother would back her daughter's decision. Mrs. Sampson had been an approving parent in many ways, including honoring her daughter's religious conversion. Her support contributed considerably to Deborah's self-confidence and amazing emotional and physical strength. Even if her mother was not present after her husband abandoned her, she saw Deborah fairly regularly, kept an eye on her health, removed her from one family's home when she felt Deborah was not happy.

Many indications of Deborah's psychological soundness are interwoven throughout her life. People frequently praised her voice as low and appealing, her manner courteous and thoughtful. She did not believe she had to be deceitful, she had enough self-esteem to dare be herself. Unlike the vast majority of women of her era, she did not think she had to get married "by hook or by crook," but considered such manipulation embarrassing, as if selling herself to the highest bidder.

She was able to live alone and enjoy her own company, an ability usually found in men and women at ease with themselves. To a remarkable degree she also was able to face the unpleasant and the disagreeable without subterfuge or evasion. When she raised a gun to kill a hawk, her little sister was horrified. Deborah assured her that women needed courage "bigger than a grain of mustard seed" in order to live on a farm.

When Deborah was twenty years old she felt confident enough to adopt her own church, defying her mother and Benjamin

Thomas, the deacon with whose family she had lived for eight years. These character traits add up to a woman of integrity and valor who possessed a solid sense of self. Dr. Betty Thompson, a physician, in a personal communication to Herman Mann described Deborah well in observing she possessed "a self that was bigger than her ego."

The race to the top of the hill also implies Deborah loved her father dearly in the early years before his desertion and supposed death. Apparently she had no difficulty in experiencing the "love affair" all healthy little girls face with their fathers, preparing them for the man to come later in their lives. She was able to maintain this feeling for a few years at the height of the oedipal period, from the ages of three to five. A hiatus is suggested by the fact that after climbing to the summit of the hill in her dream, she rested at the top.

Like dreams, our earliest memories are extremely important in telegraphing the voice of the unconscious. Recollected smells also are significant. They inform us that our most primitive emotions are operative at the time of an original experience. One of Deborah's earliest memories was of her father hugging her close as she inhaled the fragrance of tobacco and sometimes rum on his breath. This is called a "screen memory," which compresses and stands for many similar episodes of childhood. This particular memory suggests the deep and passionate love of a little girl for her father.

Much as it may seem a contradiction, a normal heterosexual development is implied in what appears to be the major identifications that led Deborah to enlist in the army. The early loving relationship with both parents intimated in the dream gave her a good start toward feminine identification. This occurred despite Deborah's choice of a conventionally masculine career, which lasted only a year-and-a-half. She possessed a healthy identification with her father as well as her brothers, in particular her dead brother Robert Shurtliff Sampson, whose name she took as she enlisted in the army. Because he died just before she was born, she never knew him. But she did sense her mother's deep loss.

Deborah was also heavily influenced by her beloved French grandmother, a woman of intelligence, elegance and beauty. Her grandmother's heroines were Joan of Arc and Deborah, the woman warrior of biblical history, for whom Deborah Sampson was named. Most important, her identification with these two famous women showed she did not identify primarily with male soldiers but with *women posing as men*. The two women warriors idolized by Deborah's grandmother helped serve as role models for Deborah's emotional development. As a result, her psychosexual development followed a far more normal path than a child whose most significant identifications are with people of the opposite sex.

The race to the top of the hill "the better to see the beauty below" indicates not only that Deborah viewed this early period with insight but also that she enjoyed her childhood happiness, in particular her "love affair" with her father. The dream holds the quality of being in love. Children who lose their parents at an early age are apt to continue to idealize them, as the missing parent becomes unavailable in adolescence and cannot be cut down to size through comparison with other adults. Although some idealization is implied, a scene viewed from a distance during a dream generally represents objectivity. The fact that Deborah looks down from the hill shows she viewed this period of her childhood objectively—and in reality it occurred pretty much as she pictured it.

Suddenly, shockingly, the serenity of the dream setting disappears. The azure sky becomes veiled in darkness, Deborah is overcome with grief. The shock, as well as the color black—the designated color of mourning—undoubtedly refers to the desertion of her father. As symbolized by the stench of sulphur, Deborah literally felt herself in hell when her beloved father forsook her. There is a depressive cast to the dream, reminiscent of the end of a love affair.

Although these feelings occur in all normal five-year-olds when disillusioned by the parent of the opposite sex, the horror of real life events heightened Deborah's experiences a thousandfold. Her grandmother had just died and shortly after Deborah's mother placed her in the care of an aunt. The little girl must have felt closer to despair than she ever would again. She had lost in one fell swoop three of the most important people in her life—her mother, her father and her loving grandmother.

As represented in the dream by the roaring seas, Deborah and her mother were both in a rage at Jonathan Sampson's desertion. If they could, they would have seized his ship and smashed it themselves upon the rocks. Their wrath probably extended to all men, as more than one ship is destroyed in the dream. With her mother furious at her husband, the daughter felt justified in her anger and vengefulness, strengthening both her self-confidence and wish for revenge.

Deborah showed a bolstering of her ego the average girl does not possess, at the height of mourning for her father as lover. Most little girls learn they have no sexual right to their father and this helps them eventually give him up. But Deborah was supported in her rage by her mother and thus felt entitled to revenge. This sense of entitlement also supported her in the quest for retaliation by joining the army.

In smashing her father against the rocks in the nightmare, Deborah was attempting to kill him off psychologically to avoid the pain and rage precipitated by his loss. But the maneuver failed, he had loomed too large in her affections to disappear without severe emotional consequences. Instead, he returned larger than life by way of her nightmares in adolescence—the time during which unfinished emotional business clamors for resolution. Because her early nightmares were so repetitive we know they failed to resolve her problems though as is their function they at least provided partial release of her deeply buried wishes and fantasies. We may speculate the nightmare recurred periodically until she enlisted in the army, then disappeared.

In the next part of the dream a hideous serpent writhed its body toward her. In the sense of "the return of the repressed," that psychological principle stated by Freud whereby disowned feelings surge toward surfacing in the conscious mind, Deborah found her father again, this time in the form of the frightful serpent. He stood for the phallic father who deserted little Deborah before she could work out her normal sexual struggles.

The size of the serpent represents how large her father's penis, or any other phallus she might have seen, appeared to Deborah as a little girl. It also reflects the enormity of her unresolved rage at her father and how powerful it loomed in her psyche. It is evident how bitterly she felt about his abandonment for she pictured him as a snake—that classic symbol of the betrayer, beginning with the Garden of Eden. The serpent left a trail of blood, representing once more the legacy of the bleeding wounds her father left behind. When she was bloodily wounded in battle, this reawakened the earlier psychological wounds—far more devastating than the physical ones.

Next in the nightmare, Deborah ran to her room, which suggests she again tried to withdraw or regress to "mother's little girl." But as Jeremiah of biblical days wails, "Is there no balm in Gilead? Is there no physician there?" Her mother had sent her away. The terror of this heartbroken child with no psychological retreats of any kind must have been acute. In the dream her defenses were shattered, no matter how fast she ran the serpent slithered behind, intent on attacking and killing her—before she could kill him.

When she reached a place she envisioned as safe, her own room, Deborah found the huge serpent coiled up inside, his body almost filling the room. This image graphically depicts the degree of grief and rage that crowded the psyche of the abandoned child. As well as the enormity of her unresolved love-hate feelings for her cruel father.

Nightmares frequently contain hidden references to an actual life event too painful to recall consciously. The image of the serpent "flicking his tongue wildly" could refer to a trauma conceivably experienced by Deborah when she was a little child. An exhibitionist, possibly even her father in one of his drunken states, might have exposed his genitalia to her while masturbating or running naked through the house on his way to the outdoor toilet. It is difficult to imagine where else she could have received such an image.

As symbolized by the "balls of fire," which frequently stand for both rage and sexual desire in a dream, such sights of her father could have thrown her into deep terror. Since she tried to scream for help in the dream but could emit no sound, we may conjecture Deborah could not call for assistance because unconsciously she was excited, as well as terrorized, by seeing her father naked. It is the rare home where a child does not once in a while glimpse her parents unclothed.

Possibly of even greater importance is the image of the bull as he rushes at Deborah and tries to gore her with his horns. This act, duplicated by the fish that attempts to strike her with his tail, suggests Deborah's father or some other male adult tried to rape her when she was very young. If so, he did not succeed in the rape.

In the dream as he chased her Deborah struck him with such fury that the bull dissolved into the ground. But her terror ran so deep it was not absolved by fighting off the attacker. The snake would remain as symbol of one of the deepest fears in her life.

The next part of her nightmare contains the core of its resolution as well as the master plan for Deborah's valiant army stint. A voice says, "Arise, stand on your feet, gird yourself, and prepare to encounter your enemy." These words, spoken to Deborah by herself, are further indication of her courage, soon to become apparent in her acts as part of the Continental Army.

Words in a dream practically always are repetitions of those heard or read by the dreamer. We can assume that some strong and respected person in Deborah's past, perhaps her mother, father, grandmother or preacher, encouraged her to stand up for herself and fight her own battles.

The injunction also may have been inspired by a philosophy highly significant in her life, namely seventeenth-century British philosopher John Locke's belief it was the right of man to overthrow a government that took his money or property without consent. England had taken, without Deborah's consent, her most important "property," her father, and she felt justified in attempting to help defeat the British government.

Deborah also would have felt it was the right of a woman to overthrow whoever might take her body without consent. Ever since her father was reported to have died in England, conceivably Deborah fought off the enemy rapist each time she raised her musket against a British soldier. By winning out over the villainous British and unconsciously also her father, she conquered evil. A voice in a dream is also a representative of the conscience. In Deborah's nightmare she gives herself permission to stand up for her rights, fight the most important battle of her life.

During the nightmare Deborah jumped on her bed when

she could find no weapon for her defense. The missing weapon implies that as a little girl she looked on the penis as a weapon, that she felt naked and vulnerable without one. This interpretation seems confirmed by the incident with her Uncle Simeon when she was four-and-a-half years old as she asked if she could be his cabin boy and, in response, he "roared with laughter." The deeply humiliated Deborah may well have created her wish to master this trauma by cross-dressing as a male. Symbolically, she would then possess her own penis and no one ever again could humiliate her.

When the serpent went after Deborah "as if to swallow her," she managed to find a bludgeon, a phallic substitute, at her feet. This last minute "rescue" suggests that late in the genital period she was able to identify with her father, or perhaps an older brother, which added to her storehouse of strength.

The dream also confirms that Deborah's identifications were primarily feminine. The masculine identification she assumed for a year and a half was not lasting, it had simply served its hidden purpose to get even with the man who had hurt her in childhood. When, as happened twice during the war, Deborah discovered she was regarded as a handsome warrior with whom a young woman fell in love, she fled the scene at once, wanted no part of their passion. We might wonder if all wars were not an attempt to get even with the hated father or mother, brother or sister—all of these early, important persons in our lives.

Deborah's fear that the serpent would swallow her infers that if she had not acted out her self-cure of joining the army, she might have been consumed by the conflict with her father, perhaps would never lead the normal family life blueprinted by her happy earlier experiences.

When the serpent slithered away for a moment, it seemed as though Deborah's masculine identifications might be successful at keeping her rage and grief at bay. But then the monster returned, trying to use his tail as he flailed against her. Then the tail turned into a fish as weapon. Deborah used three symbols for the penis as weapon: the tail of the serpent, the fish and the horns of the raging bull. This confirms the conjecture that at some point in her early life she believed the penis a weapon with which the man attacks the woman sexually—the belief of children who have seen their parents in sexual intercourse and can explain the act in no other way.

The dream also corroborates by way of repetition the speculation that because of sexual trauma the adult male penis was a source of terror to Deborah. It further hints that without the previously postulated sexual shock, she might have been able to tolerate the loss of her father without developing a neurosis, or needing to resort to that drastic measure of cure, her army service.

The next part of the dream concerns Deborah's repetitive and continually failing psychological efforts to kill her father. She flails away at the serpent until he falls in pieces on the ground but then the severed parts reunite in the shape of a giant bull. The symbol she chooses for her father is huge, sexual and overpowering. The bull tries to gore her with his horns. But she strikes him again and this time he dissolves into pieces. Once more we encounter Deborah's deep emotional strength as she temporarily becomes able to pulverize the strong passions precipitated by her father's defection.

Because she still loved her father and needed him to complete her development, she tried to resuscitate him. But the repressed wish to kill won out once more as he dissolved into the pool of jelly, all that was left of the bull. The jelly possibly refers to the semen ejaculated by the previously postulated rapist or by the exhibitionist masturbating to orgasm. If either of these assaults occurred it could possibly cause her love for her father to dissolve into nothingness. But more important, the pool probably stands for Deborah's fear of regression into despair when her father left home. She was terrified that without him she would disappear into nothingness.

The thought of finding nothing where once there had been something ran through Deborah's psychological history. Becoming as nothing was how she felt when she ran away from panic. When she joined the army her hidden terror was so overwhelming that, as she later told Mann, she "felt at first like shrinking into a nothing like a fly rolled up in the fold of a dark curtain."

The pain of her loss and despair had become so excruciating she both feared and wished she would shrink into nothingness. Only if she were a "nothing" could she find peace. Despite her strength to resist its pull, the traumatic loss of her father, which brought on the loss of her mother, too, as Deborah was farmed out, threatened at an early age the collapse of her world. Her ambivalence toward her father, who started the pain, is evident in the dream as she repeatedly brings him back to life, then tries to kill him off. The conflict seemed intolerable, it woke her from the nightmare each time she unconsciously summoned it.

Deborah's unresolved problems were vividly traced in this telling dream. It also laid out their solution according to the philosophy of John Locke, who stated it is the right of man to overthrow a government that seizes his property or money without consent. In a sense Locke spoke for Deborah, gave her permission to enlist in the army, to discharge her rage and avenge her father's desertion of his family. She was saying to him, "I will not desert my country as you deserted your family."

After she accomplished the phenomenal feat of going to war, Deborah's psychological difficulties appeared to be appeased. She no longer had to maintain the illusion she was a man in order to survive.

She had joined the army not only to wage war against the British enemy but the war within her heart that ate away at her soul. As she could express her fury on the battlefield, fight to kill the enemy, she eased her guilt and death wishes directed at the father who had abandoned her.

Daddy's little girl finally had her revenge and could let go of the buried rage of childhood.

LOVE AT LONG LAST

Deborah realized part of her did not want to go home. She was not ready to face her mother who, she feared, would never understand why she deserted her to fight in the army.

She needed time to return to her role as a woman, after thinking and acting like a man for a year and a half. She also wanted to hold on for a while longer to the image of herself as a soldier of the Continental Army.

Her father would have been proud of her, he would have praised her for showing the world a woman could fight as valiantly as a man, she thought. He would have lauded her courage in living under constant fear of discovery.

She had always felt close to an uncle, Zebulon Waters, the husband of her mother's sister, Alice. The Waters lived in Stoughton, which bordered on Sharon, eighteen miles west of Middleborough, not far from the lake where bog iron had been discovered during the war.

Deborah decided to go straight to the Waters' house. She believed they would understand what she had done for her country. After arriving in Boston on November 1, 1783, she headed for her uncle's farm on Bay Road. At one time an Indian path, it was now a stagecoach route connecting Massachusetts Bay with Narragansett Bay which extends into Rhode Island.

When she reached the two-story house, built in 1730, she knocked on the door. Her Aunt Alice opened it. Deborah was still in uniform, regimental coat and hat, her haversack slung over her shoulders.

"Yes?" said her aunt, not recognizing her.

Deborah pulled off the plumed hat, her curly blond hair tumbling dramatically about her face. "Aunt Alice, it's me, Deborah," she declared, wanting her aunt to recognize her.

Her aunt gasped, drew Deborah into the house, kissed her and asked, "What are you doing in that uniform, child?"

"I was in the army, Aunt Alice," she said in her quiet voice.

"Zeb, come here quick!" her aunt called out.

Deborah's Uncle Zeb, tall, gaunt, dependable, walked in from the kitchen. Seeing Deborah, he rushed over and hugged her. Then he stood back, stared at the uniform asked, "What's this all about?"

During supper she described how she had fought Tories, Indians and redcoats, lived in forests in fear of bears, wolves and snakes, suffered frostbite, sometimes went hungry for days, risked infection as she removed a musket ball from her thigh, caught the malignant fever and nearly died, almost drowned twice, once near Peekskill, the second time in the waters just south of New York City.

"Does your mother know all this?" her uncle asked.

"No," she said. "And I can't tell her just yet. I thought maybe you'd let me stay here for a while to help you out. Could you use a pair of extra hands?"

"If they're yours," said her favorite uncle.

She felt fortunate the men she knew were so understanding— Dr. Binney, General Paterson and her uncle. She made a request, pleaded, "If anyone asks the name of your new farm hand, please tell them Ephraim Sampson." She chose the name of another brother. Her mother preferred boys and it would take a while for Deborah to return to feeling like a woman.

"Aren't you going to dress like a woman?" her aunt asked.

"After a while," Deborah assured her.

"Let her get used to the old life first," her sensitive uncle advised. "It'll take time to recover from what she's been through."

As Deborah once again fed cows, pigs and chickens, she thought of how she had exchanged these chores for an existence that offered far more adventure and thrills, but brimmed with danger every minute of the day and night. She had taken many chances with her life, not only the times she could have been killed in battle but seeking out self-destructive acts like volunteering to go with the Indians in Shenandoah Valley. They could just as easily have scalped or burned her at the stake as let her live.

She sensed she had no choice, she wanted to avenge her father's abandonment and the abuse suffered at the hands of others, then pick up the normal development so abruptly truncated at the age of five. She did not wholly know how but she had absorbed her rage and need for revenge by serving in the army. Now she wanted to be a complete woman again. As in the start of her recurring nightmare, the deer would graze, the birds would carol and all would be right with the world.

Deborah had read in the *Boston Gazette* a report of General Washington's "Farewell Orders" issued November 2 at Rocky Hill, Jersey, his temporary new headquarters near Princeton where Congress was convening. With his customary consideration, General Washington thanked the soldiers, saying, "From their good sense and prudence, he," referring to himself as the commander in chief, "anticipates the happiest consequences; and while he congratulated them on the glorious occasion which renders their services in the field no longer necessary, he wishes to express the strong obligations he feels himself under for the assistance he had received from every class—and in every instance."

He also thanked "the non-commissioned officers and private soldiers for their extraordinary patience and suffering, as well as their invincible fortitude in action." Deborah felt a singular pride at these remarks of her hero, knowing they were meant for her as much as for the men in the army.

The *Gazette* also noted General Washington was planning to ride to Mount Vernon for Christmas with his wife, the first time he would see his home in eight years. Deborah was happy for the general that he, too, would soon be at home, pictured him walking about his grand estate, as she had once done, thanks to Dr. Binney.

It had been almost two years since she and her mother had seen each other. Frightened at the possibility of her mother's anger or outright rejection, Deborah bided her time.

One day, like Lady Macbeth, who "screwed her courage to a sticking post," Deborah suddenly found herself in a farmer's cart setting out for Plymouth.

Her mother recognized her immediately, burst into tears the moment Deborah walked through the door. "I thought you were dead! Why didn't you write?" she asked between sobs.

Then, before waiting for an answer, she asked, "What are you doing in men's clothes?" There was alarm in her voice.

"It's a long story, mother." Deborah felt gratified that at last someone had recognized her in men's clothes, though *Wouldn't you know it would be my mother?* she thought wryly.

She sketched in words what had happened to her, omitting her most dangerous experiences. She did not want to upset her mother any more than necessary.

"Why didn't you come here when you returned to Massachusetts?" her mother reproached her.

"I needed time to get the courage to tell you what I had done." Deborah replied with the truth.

"You needed courage for that? After all you'd been through?" Her mother stared at her in amazement.

Deborah laughed. "Sometimes it's harder to face a mother than the enemy on a battlefield," she said. "You can't fire a musket at a mother when you feel she is oppressing you."

"Deborah, that's not fair!" her mother exclaimed.

Deborah realized her mother was right, the oppressive mother was in her head, not the real mother. "It *isn't* fair," she admitted. "I love you very much. I know now that you didn't give me away when I was five-and-a-half because you hated me—even though it seemed in my little-girl mind that had to be the reason."

"You always were a strong-willed child," said her mother with a smile. Then added with admiration, "Though I never thought your spirit would take you as far as it did."

"You forgive me?" Deborah asked, just to make sure.

"It all turned out for the best," said her mother. "You didn't get killed and the army officers didn't punish you. God was good to you."

God *had* been very good to her, she thought, though some of His representatives on earth were not so kind. She learned that the Third Baptist Church in Middleborough had expelled her while she was away. She read the records of the church dated September 3, 1782 that stated:

Considered the case of Deborah Sampson, a member of this Church, who last Spring was accused of Dressing in men's Clothes, and inlisting as a soldier in the army and altho she was not convicted, yet was strongly suspected of being guilty and for sometime before behaved very loose and unchristian like, and at last left our parts in a secret manner and it is not known among us where she is gone; and after considerable discourse it appeared that as several bretheren had labored with her before she went away without obtaining satisfaction, concluded it is the church's Duty to withdraw fellowship untill she returns and makes Christian satisfaction.

They referred to the time she enlisted as "Timothy Thayer." She had behaved unwisely when she borrowed Samuel Leonard's suit, enlisted locally, then enjoyed two drinks at Sproat Tavern which unloosed her tongue and singing voice. She did not blame those who were horrified by her masquerade as a man. At that time she did not understand her need to rebel. It had been a delayed adolescent rebellion. Without it, she never would have embarked on what she believed her calling.

Her mother told her the news of her brothers and sisters, most of whom were married and raising large families. Deborah, who had helped bring up the three youngest Thomas boys, was eager to meet her own nieces and nephews, hold them in her arms. Her mother asked if she were going to stay in Stoughton. She answered, "For a while. I'm happy there."

Deborah then asked about the man her mother had wanted her to marry. He finally had given up on Deborah. After trying to find her at West Point he married someone else. Deborah felt relieved, knowing her mother could no longer urge her to marry him. But she also had a small twinge of regret, the fear no man ever again might ask for her hand in marriage.

She was not to feel regretful for long. One evening her aunt invited to dinner the son of a farmer who lived two miles away in Sharon. His name was Benjamin Gannett, Jr. He was six years older than Deborah. His ancestors had settled in that region, decade after decade his family eked out a livelihood from almost the same patch of earth.

Benjamin, like Deborah, was descended from Priscilla and John Alden. His mother, Mary Copeland, was their great-great-granddaughter. Another ancestor of Benjamin's was Matthew Gannett, born in England in 1618, one of the early settlers of New England. He lived first in Hingham, Massachusetts, then purchased land in Scituate in January 1651. Matthew Gannett's grandson, Benjamin Gannett, Sr., born in 1728, married Mary Copeland in 1750. She was the daughter of Jonathan Copeland of Bridgewater, who moved to Stoughton, then Sharon.

Benjamin now visited Deborah every evening after work ended on his father's farm. If she had to go to town on an errand for her aunt or uncle, Benjamin offered to ride her on his horse. She sat behind him, arms clasped around his waist. If she wanted to stay home and sew or read, he sat quietly by her side.

He never criticized her for wearing men's clothing, accepted her as she was. He even admired her revolutionary hat and coat.

Deborah needed this above all else, to be accepted for herself, not judged by someone's idea of what a woman should be like.

One spring evening she walked into the parlor wearing a dress. She had made it secretly, perhaps because Benjamin had given her permission to dress however she chose. Her aunt, uncle and Benjamin stared at her, surprised and pleased.

"No more uniform," she said. "I buried it."

Her uncle laughed, then commented, "With proper funeral rites, I hope."

"A few prayers," she answered. "It served me well."

When Benjamin asked her to marry him, it felt far different from her first suitor's proposal. He kissed her on the lips, the first kiss she had received from a man in the twenty-four years of her life, except for the kisses her father bestowed on her cheek before the age of five-and-a-half.

Benjamin's ardent kisses sent a ripple of pleasure through her body. She would lift her head for a second kiss. She inhaled the farm worker's rugged scent she had once loved while in her father's arms. Benjamin and she sat locked together at times on the large parlor chair, silent in their bliss as life took on a new dimension.

Deborah felt like someone blind from birth suddenly given the gift of sight. How could she not have known such ecstasy existed? She realized if she had, she probably could not have survived the army, without giving in to some man's charm.

She had done her part to free her country. She had wished for revenge on her father for leaving his family and on her uncle Simeon for his scorn when she offered to serve him as a young girl. She had unfettered herself from such childish wishes. She finally felt free to become wife and mother.

"SHE ALMOST MADE THE GUN TALK"

According to Sharon town records, "Intentions of Marriage between Benjamin Gannett Jr of Sharon, Deborah Sampson of Stoughton Entered with me ye Subscriber Octobr ye 14, 1784." They were married on April 7, 1785 at the home of Benjamin Gannett, Sr., by town clerk George Crossman.

They moved in with Benjamin's father and his second wife, sharing the farmhouse that stood near the crossing of Billings and East Streets. Perhaps Deborah felt a bit crowded living with her in-laws but the young couple remained two years. Deborah gave birth in this house to her only son, Earl, early in 1786.

After the child's birth Benjamin promptly bought their own home in Sharon on March 18, 1786, a few miles from the old Gannett farm on East Street. He paid Jeremiah Belcher thirty-four pounds, seven shillings, "lawful silver money." A daughter Mary was born in 1790 and another daughter, Patience, in 1791. Deborah, who knew what it felt to be motherless, also brought up another baby, Susann Shepard, whose mother died in September 1796 when Susann was only five days old.

For the first time Deborah Sampson Gannett became mistress of her own home. Their son Earl, who became a captain in the War of 1812, later built a spacious house at 300 East Street in Sharon for his mother and father. Deborah lived there until her death at the age of sixty-eight. By then she had enjoyed twelve grandchildren, eight of them born to Patience and Seth Gay. Deborah could feel herself a true homemaker, wife, mother and grandmother.

To the front of her new house, as part of the stone wall, she brought one enormous rock, three-and-a-half feet long and one-and-a-half feet wide, from the old Gannett farm. The rock was marked by a cellar hole, overgrown with weeds on property belonging to the Sharon Fish and Game Club. Deborah also planted in the front yard a sapling from a willow tree brought from the yard of her birthplace in Plympton.

The house Earl built for his parents on East Street was owned, as of 1980, by Daniel Arguimbau, a descendant of Alice Southworth, the second wife of Governor William Bradford. A marker on the outside reads: DEBORAH SAMPSON GANNETT HOUSE 1813. The house has been modernized but several of the bedroom floors still preserve the original planks and the corner of one closet boasts an original beam.

Soon after Deborah's discharge from the army a New York newspaper published a story about her, copied by the Massachusetts papers, from facts reportedly obtained through the officers at West Point. It was then that Herman Mann, printer and sometimes editorial writer for the *Village Register* in Dedham, Massachusetts, became interested in writing the story of her life.

He persuaded Deborah to let him interview her at length for a book about her war experiences. It was called *The Female Review, Memoirs of an American Young Lady.* The book was printed in 1797 in Dedham by Nathaniel and Benjamin Heaton "for the author."

Mann arranged for a list of subscribers to pay the costs, promised Deborah a share of the profits from sales. He is reported to have embellished some of the facts she gave him and later researchers, such as Pauline Moody and Charles Bricknell, spent years trying to separate fact from fiction. Mann's book is written in a rather pompous, moralistic style believed to be his, not Deborah's.

Joseph Stone of Framingham, Massachusetts, painted Deborah's picture for the frontispiece of the book. She bought for the occasion a new dress quite feminine in style, of white lawn with a high-waisted blue sash and ruffled collar. Her blond hair curled over her shoulders and she wore a choker of beads. The painting, seven inches by ten inches, showed her framed by flags and patriotic symbols. It was done in oils on paper to save the cost of canvas. Unfortunately it is believed a very uncomplimentary likeness but the only one in existence. It hangs at the John Brown House of the Rhode Island Historical Society in Providence. The Dedham Historical Society has a copper engraving of the portrait.

Mann later edited his book in another version. After he died his son added to the manuscript. Neither of these two books was made public but both are in possession of the Dedham Historical Society.

The original book by Mann appeared in a second published version in 1866 when the Reverend John Adams Vinton edited it, adding footnotes that contained new facts and corrections. His edition was published by J.K. Wiggin and William Parson Lunt in Boston. It was titled *The Female Review, Life of Deborah Sampson, The Female Soldier in the War of the Revolution*, with an introduction and notes by Vinton.

Various articles and sections of books have been written about the life of Deborah, some with embellishments, some contradicting each other, all handed over to the generations by her descendants. Pauline Moody's forty-eight page booklet entitled *Massachusetts' Deborah Sampson*, privately printed, is the most authentic, published after ten years of research. Charles Bricknell also spent years of research on Deborah's life.

Whether Deborah ever received money from the sale of Mann's book is not known. But she did profit both financially and psychologically from a second idea of Mann's. In 1802, when Deborah was forty-two, he persuaded her to deliver a "narrative," or "oration," at a series of towns and cities throughout Massachusetts, Rhode Island and New York.

Again she became a pioneer. She embarked on a lecture tour as she broke convention, daring to speak in public of her enlistment as a man in the Continental Army during an era women sat at home sewing, spinning or churning butter. But it was not only convention Deborah broke, she overcame her own inhibitions as well. Standing on the platform, all eyes upon her, she must have felt at least a flush of pleasure.

For the first time she was able to gratify in acceptable fashion the exhibitionistic needs she had hidden from herself for so long, thus enhancing her psychological development at the age of forty-two. Not only in the military did she prove she was truly a heroine.

Traveling alone, keeping her own itemized expenses, she arranged her performances after she arrived in each town. She journeyed in private carriages, stagecoaches carrying the mail, once took a six-day wagon trip over rutted roads. The tour lasted from March 22, 1802 through the spring of 1803. Between engagements she spent weeks at home.

She kept a diary of her travels, describing briefly her vicissitudes and social life. She delivered the same lecture each time, speaking from memory. Mann wrote the lecture for her in much the same flowery, pompous style as his book, full of literary allusions but containing little about her war experiences. Despite her usual fortitude, she was apparently unable to speak before audiences from her own heart.

Deborah made her first appearance in Boston, recalling no doubt the time she marched through the city on her way to enlist. She dressed in the Liberty Square rooming house of Robert Williams, putting on a newly made uniform that replicated the one worn by the soldiers of the Continental Army. Then she traveled by carriage to the Federal Street Theatre. Boston newspapers, including *The Columbian Centinel and Massachusetts Federalist*, advertised her program.

She shared billing on four successive evenings, starting March 22, 1802 with productions of *King Henry IV*, *The Will: or A School for Daughters* and *Columbus: or America Discovered*. Wearing her blue and white uniform and armed with a musket, she paced through twenty-seven of the manual of arms maneuvers at the command of an officer before presenting her "oration." One critic wrote, "She almost made the gun talk."

Deborah apologized for what she had done as a woman—the voice of Mann, no doubt—when she said, "My achievements are a breach in the decorum of my sex, unquestionably." But she briefly found her own voice as she described her war experiences: "I must frankly confess I recollect them with a kind of satisfaction." She demurely added a gesture to propriety, "Which no one can better conceive and enjoy than him who, recollecting the good intentions of a bad deed, lives to see and to correct any indecorum of his life."

Deborah explained why she had gone to war: "Know then that my juvenile mind early became inquisitive to understand why man should march out tranquilly, or in a paroxysm of rage against his fellow man, to butcher, or be butchered." Why, indeed, she may have wondered, did her father indulge in his drunken rages against his own family?

She continued: "But most of all, my mind became agitated with the enquiry—why a nation, separated from us by an ocean more than three thousand miles in extent, should endeavor to enforce on us plans of subjugation, the most unnatural in themselves, unjust, inhuman, in their operations, and unpracticed even by the uncivilized savages of the wilderness? [meaning the American Indian.] We indeed originated from her, as from a parent, and had, perhaps, continued to this period in subjection to her mandates, had we not discovered that this, her romantic, avaricious and cruel disposition extended to murder, after having bound the slave. I only seemed to want the license to become one of the severest avengers of the wrong."

In a sense Deborah had been bound in psychological slavery by her father's treatment of her. Although he had sailed three thousand miles away, deserting his family forever (what kind of man would abandon eight small children and a wife?) the emotional damage precipitated by his loss stayed within Deborah and continued to overwhelm her until she was able to avenge the wrong he had done.

Deborah added that in Massachusetts "for several years I looked on scenes of havoc, rapacity and devastation, as one looks on a drowning man, on the conflagration of a city, without being able to extend the rescuing hand to butchered relatives and friends, towns set afire."

Here Deborah may have referred to the helplessness she experienced while taking in the psychological havoc inflicted by her father on her mother and seven siblings, in addition to the slaughter and burning of homes brought on by the British.

She concluded: "Wrought upon at length, you may say, by an enthusiasm and phrenzy that could brook no control—I burst the tyrant bonds, which held my sex in awe, and clandestinely, or by stealth, grasped an opportunity, which custom and the world seemed to deny, as a natural privilege. And whilst poverty, hunger, nakedness, cold and disease had dwindled the American Armies to a handful—whilst universal terror and dismay ran through the camps . . . did I throw off the soft bailments of my sex, and assume those of the warrior, already prepared for battle."

There is quite a contrast between the pontifical language of the address and the entries in her diary, written from the heart, as she tells of her reception by audiences, of her longing to see her children, and the fatigue and illnesses she suffered along the way. In the diary we see the true Deborah Sampson, uncontaminated by the pedantic efforts of Mann.

Her entry on May 5, 1802, from Providence is unstudied, simple and filled with a childlike candor: "When I entered the Hall, I must say I was much pleased at the appearance of the audience. It appeared from almost every countenance that they were full of unbelief—I mean, in Regard to my being the person that served in the Revolutionary Army.

"Some of them which I happened to overhear Swore that I was a lad of not more than eighteen years of age. I sat some time in my chair before I rose to Deliver my Address. When I did, I think I may say with much candor I applauded the people for their serious attention and peculiar Respect, especially the Ladies."

The entry of June 28, written at home straight from her

motherly heart, reads: "I tarried with my family the most of the month of June, much agitated in mind—anxious to persevere in my journey—tho' a heart filled with pain when I Realized parting with my three Dear Children and other friends. I may say four Dear children—my Dear Little Susann Shepard whom I took at five days old at her mother's Death."

One of the entries between July 10 to July 30, during which time she visited George Webb, the old army captain who headed her light infantry division, read: "Hired Horse and chaise, went on to Holden to Capt. George Webb's, taried there until 29th. Exhibited in Holden before a Very Respectable Circle."

Deborah showed she was becoming weary on September 7 in Schenectady. In contrast to the pleasure she felt while traveling in the army, she was now homesick: "This city is situated on the West Branch of the Mohock [Mohawk] River. It is a gloomy way indeed from Albany to this place."

October 10: "The homesickness continues. I arrived in Albany to go to Capt. Keelers. Very much fatigued indeed. I have a gloomy ride this Day through barron sands over pine and scrub plains, one of these plains is 16 miles in length. Nothing in the least inviting to the weary traveller."

October 11: "I this Day am taken very sick with the toothake and ague in my face." Her physical state seems to complement her mental one.

October 14: "I am quite unwell. I have Done no business to advantage for this long time. Only spend money. O, how gloomy are my feelings! no prospect of anything but trouble before me—a great distance from my Native home among entire strangers."

Her biggest triumph occurred as guest for a month at the home of her West Point friend, General John Paterson. He lived in Lisle, New York, where he served as a judge in Broome County and member of the New York State legislature. The reunion was warm between the general of the First Brigade and the woman who had successfully passed as a soldier for a year-and-a-half, part of the time as his aide-de-camp. She might never have been discovered as a woman had not a Philadelphia surgeon saved her life in his hospital.

She wrote on November 11: "I arrived at Judge Paterson's at Lisle. This respectable family treated me with every mark of Distinction and friendship, and likewise all the people Did the same. I Really want for Words to Express my Gratitude. They seemed to unite in hearty congratulations with my old friend Judge Paterson on our happy meeting.

"Thus I spent my time as agreeably as one can, considering my Circumstances. But oh, how often is the mind harrowed up by recollection! to think of myself so far from my Dear Children, no opportunity of hearing them, and God only knows when I shall be so happy as to see them."

Delighted as Deborah was to meet once again her former officer and mentor, her army career could not now compete in importance with her love for her children. She missed them deeply, despite the kindness of the former general and his friends.

She wrote on December 5, "Threatened with the fever—a violent pain in my head and left side. Sent for Dr. Huntington, my fever is seated on me." Dr. Huntington sent her home at this point and there she slowly recovered from what was evidently a deep-seated flu.

The following year Deborah learned that General Paterson had been elected to the United States Congress. He would eventually be instrumental in securing for her a much-needed pension of four dollars a month from the federal government for her services in the Revolutionary War. Her monies from her lectures scarcely brought in enough to cover expenses at the Gannett household.

The annals of Sharon praise the Gannett men for their liberal contributions of cattle and grain throughout the Revolution. But their families, along with those of thousands of other farmers, were now deeply affected by postwar inflation as prices of food and clothing rose drastically.

Deborah realized she had to take some action to obtain money for the care of her children. The farm products did not yield enough, nor did her lectures.

"YOUR GRANDMOTHER WAS A SOLDIER!"

Deborah had stated in her lectures that she had not received "one farthing" for her service in the army. She had petitioned the Commonwealth of Massachusetts for money owed her in January 1792. Her petition read:

To His Excellency the Governor, the Honorable Senate, and the Honourable House of Representatives, in General Court assembled, this Eleventh day of January, 1792.

The Memorial of Deborah Gannett Humbly Sheweth that your Memorialist from zeal for the good of her country was induc'd, and by the name of Robert Shurtliff did, on May 20, 1782, Inlist as a

Soldier in the Continental Service, for Three Years, into the 4th Regiment, Col. Shepard's (afterwards Col. Jackson's) in Capt. George Webb's Com'y. & was mustered at Worcester, by Capt. Eliphalet Thorp of Dedham, the 23rd of the same Month, & went to the Camp, under the Command of Sergeant Gambel, & was constant & faithful in doing Duty with other soldiers, & was engag'd with the Enemy at Tarry Town, New York, & was wounded there by the enemy, & continued in Service until discharged, by General Henry Knox at West Point October 25, 1783. Your Memorialist has made some Application to receive pay for her services in the Army, but being a Female, & not knowing the proper steps to take to get pay for her services, has hitherto not received one farthing for her services, whether it has been occasioned by the fault of Officers in making up the Rolls, or whether Effrican Hamblin pay master to the 4th regiment, has carried off the papers, &c., your Memorialist cannot say: but your Memorialist prays this Honourable Court to consider the Justness of her Claim, & grant her pay as a good soldier, and your Memorialist as in Duty bound shall ever pray.

This petition was presented to the Massachusetts House of Representatives and then referred to a committee consisting of Dr. William Eustis of Boston (later to become governor), Benjamin Hitchborn of Dorchester and James Sproat of Middleborough. The committee reported favorably on the petition and the following resolve was passed:

Whereas it appears to this Court that the said Deborah Gannett inlisted under the name of Robert Shurtliff, in Captain Webb's company in the 4th Massachusetts Regiment on May 20, 1782, and did actually perform the duty of a Soldier in the late army of the United States to the 23rd day of October, 1783, for which she received no compensation:

And whereas it further appears that the said Deborah exhibited an extraordinary instance of female heroism by discharging the duties of a faithful, gallant soldier, and at the same time preserving the virtue & chastity of her sex unsuspected & unblemished, & was discharged from the service with a fair & honorable character, Therefore

Resolved That the treasurer of this Commonwealth be & he hereby is directed to issue his note to the said Deborah for the sum of Thirty four pounds bearing interest from October 23, 1783.

The thirty-four pounds amounted to a little over one hundred dollars for her eighteen months of service. The document was approved by John Hancock, governor of Massachusetts, and signed by D. Cobb, Speaker of the House of Representatives, and Samuel Phillips, President.

On file in the office of the Secretary of the Commonwealth of Massachusetts is a statement by Henry Jackson, a former colonel in the Continental Army, dated "Boston, Aug. 1, 1786," which states:

To whom it may concern.

This may Certify that Robert Shurtliff was a Soldier in my Regiment in the Continental army for the town of Uxbridge in the Commonwealth of Massachusetts & was inlisted for the term of three years: that he had the confidence of his officers and did his duty as a faithful & good soldier, & was honorably discharged from the army of the United States.

The name "Shurtliff" which Deborah used when she enlisted has been spelled in many ways, including Shurtlieff, Shirtliff, Shurtliff and Shirtlief. In all, research showed there were twenty-two spellings that appeared in the *Massachusetts Soldiers and Sailors of the Revolutionary War.*

A subjoined certificate that accompanied the preceding paper stated:

> Dedham, Decem. 19, 1791
>
> This Certifies that Mrs. Deborah Gannett inlisted as a Soldier on May ye 20th 1782 for three years, and was Muster'd ye 23rd of ye Same Month at Worcester and sent on to Camp soon after and as I have been informed did the Duty of a Good Soldier.
>
> Pr. ELIPHT. THORP, 4th M. Regt. Muster Master
>
> N.B. Robert Shurtliff was ye name by which Mrs. Gannett inlisted and Muster'd.

Deborah had signed the receipt for her bounty money when she first entered the Army as Robert Shurtliff. The Massachusetts State Archives possesses a receipt dated "Worcester—May 23, 1782," which states, "The sum of Sixty Pounds—L. [legal]—Money as a Bounty to serve in the Continental Army for the term of three years." It also notes the bounty was "Received of Mr. Noah Taft—Chairman of Class No. 2 for the town of Uxbridge."

In the "List of Final Settlements," a volume in the office of the Secretary of the Commonwealth of Massachusetts containing the names of soldiers discharged in 1783 from the Continental Army, appears the name Robert Shurtliff. Opposite it appears the number 40066, reference to documents sent to the War Office at Washington. Unfortunately, there is no record of the moving letter Dr. Binney wrote General Paterson.

Around 1804 Deborah met a girlhood hero, Paul Revere, who had bought a copper manufacturing plant in nearby Canton. Undoubtedly he had heard of her, wanted to meet her as much as she wished to meet him. They are reported to have enjoyed a drink together occasionally at Cobb's Tavern in Sharon, the halfway stop on the Old Bay Road between Boston and Taunton.

At this time Deborah asked Revere to help her get further monies from Congress. He wrote William Eustis, the Massachusetts representative in Congress, the following letter:

Sir

Mrs. Deborah Gannett of Sharon informs me, that she had inclosed to your care a petition to Congress in favour of her. My works for manufacturing of copper, being at Canton, being but a short distance from the neighborhood where she lives, I have been induced to inquire her situation and character, since she quitted the male habit, and soldier's uniform, for the more decent apparel of her own sex, and since she has been married and become a mother. Humanity and justice obliges me to say, that every person with whom I have conversed about her, and it is not a few, speak of her as a woman of handsome talents, good morals, a dutiful wife, and an affectionate parent. She is now much out of health. She has several children, her husband is a good sort of man, 'tho of small force in business; they have a few acres of poor land which they cultivate, but they are really poor.

She told me that no doubt her ill health is in consequence of her being exposed when she did a soldier's duty, and that while in the army she was wounded.

We commonly form our idea of the person whom we hear spoken of, whom we have never seen, according as their actions are described. When I heard her spoken of as a soldier, I formed the idea of a tall, masculine female, who had a small share of understanding, without education, and one of the meanest of her sex.— When I saw and discoursed with her I was agreeably surprised to find a small, effeminate, and conversable woman, whose education entitled her to a better situation in life.

I have no doubt your humanity will prompt you to do all in your power to get her some relief. I think her case much more deserving than hundreds to whom Congress has been generous.

> I am sirs with esteem and respect
> your humble servant, Paul Revere.

Congress granted Deborah the right to be placed on the Massachusetts invalid pension roll, and she received four dollars a month, retroactive to the first of January, 1803, paid for by the Commonwealth of Massachusetts.

Two years later she wrote Revere, again asking for his help, this time in a personal way:

I would inform you that I and my son have been very sick—though in some measure better. I hope, sir, that you and your Family are all in the enjoyment of health, which is one of the greatest of blessings. My own indisposition and that of my son's causes me again to solicit your Goodness in our favor—though I with Gratitude Confess it arouses every tender feeling, & I blush at the thought that after receiving ninety and nine good turns as it were—my circumstances require that I should ask the Hundredth—the Favour that I ask is the loan of 10 dollars for a short time. As soon as I am able to ride to Boston I will make my Remittance to you. With my humble thanks for the distinguished favour—from your humble servant, Deborah Gannett.

It is sad to think that a great heroine who, along with her cohorts, was instrumental in the freeing of the colonies from the British should find it necessary to grovel for the pittance of ten dollars. Even after her children were married—Earl Bradford to Mary Clark, Patience to Seth Gay and Mary to Judson Gilbert—Deborah seemed to have little money. A few years before her death when required to list the value of everything she owned, she said the only property she possessed was her wearing apparel, worth twenty dollars.

In March 1818, Congress passed an act granting pensions of eight dollars per month to all veterans who had served continuously a minimum of nine months in the land and naval forces of the United States during the Revolution. Veterans already holding state pensions were not eligible under the act unless they relinquished their rights to the first pension. In September, Deborah petitioned Congress for money under the act. This time, however, she gave her date of enlistment as April, 1781, and said she had served at the Battle of Yorktown.

The Reverend John Adams Vinton questioned this date of enlistment, believing Herman Mann had added the Yorktown material to make Deborah's biography more dramatic, taking the description of the battle almost word for word from Dr. James Thacher's *Military Journal*. Massachusetts records prove she enlisted in 1782 and served in the army a year-and-a-half.

The date of her enlistment had no bearing, however, on whether her application was approved by Congress, as it soon was. This brought a comment from the editors of the *Village Register* in Dedham: "This extraordinary woman is now in the sixty-second year of her age. She possesses a clear understanding, and a general knowledge of passing events, is fluent in speech, and delivers her sentiments in correct language, with deliberate and measured accent, is easy in deportment, affable in her manners, robust and masculine in her appearance."

The description seems congruent with those of others, except for the portrayal of Deborah as "masculine in appearance." It seems people could not agree as to whether she looked masculine or feminine. Paul Revere depicted her as totally feminine in demeanor and behavior. Perhaps what others saw was more in the eye of the beholder than the persona of Deborah.

In 1831, four years after Deborah died at the age of sixty-eight, Benjamin Gannett then seventy-eight years old, petitioned Congress for the continuation of his wife's pension for himself, claiming her war wounds had hastened her death.

This request was introduced in Congress by John Quincy Adams, son of Abigail and John Adams, and a member of the House of Representatives. It was not acted on at the time because there was no law as of yet granting pensions to widows whose husbands had died of war wounds. But in 1836 Congress passed an act "granting half pay to widows or orphans where their husbands or fathers have died of wounds received in the military service of the United States." Benjamin Gannett again petitioned for such a pension though the act specified the widow would have had to be married to the soldier at the time of the Revolution.

Benjamin claimed heavy medical expenses due to his wife's war wound from a second musket ball that had remained imbedded in her left thigh and caused her pain over the years. He presented a physician's bill of $600 as evidence. A sympathetic Committee on Revolutionary Pensions reported to the twenty-fifth Congress on December 22, 1837:

Were there nothing peculiar in this application which distinguishes it from all other applications for pensions, the committee would at once reject the claim. But they believe they are warranted in saying that the whole history of the American Revolution records no case like this, and furnishes no other similar example of female heroism, fidelity, and courage. The petitioner does not allege that he served in the war of the Revolution, and it does not appear by any evidence in the case that such was the fact.

It is not, however to be presumed that a female who took up arms in defense of her country, who served as a common soldier for nearly three years, and fought and bled for human liberty, would, immediately after the termination of the war, connect herself for life with a Tory or a traitor. He, indeed, was honored much by being the husband of such a wife; and as he proved himself worthy of her, as he has sustained her through a long life of sickness and suffering, and as that sickness and suffering were occasioned by wounds she received and the hardships she endured in the defense of her country, and as there cannot be a parallel case in all time to come, the committee does not hesitate to grant relief.

But by that time it was too late. Benjamin Gannett died at the age of eighty-five. He had been in his grave only three weeks when the pension was granted on July 7, 1838, as Congress passed a special act for the relief of Deborah Gannett's heirs. Congress directed the Secretary of the Treasury to pay Deborah's family $466.66, the equivalent of a full pension of eighty dollars per year, from the time of Mr. Gannett's first petition until his death.

This act established a precedent. Through his heirs, Benjamin Gannett became the first man granted a pension by the United States government for military service performed by his wife.

In his book the Reverend Vinton includes an extract of a letter from the Honorable William Ellis, formerly a senator in Congress, written to the Honorable Peter Force of Washington, D. C. It is dated "Dedham, Feb. 4, 1837," and reads:

From my own acquaintance with Deborah Gannett, I can truly say that she was a woman of uncommon native intellect and force of character. It happens that I have several connections who reside in the immediate neighborhood where Mrs. Gannett lived and died and I have never heard from them, or any other source, any suggestion against the character of this heroine. Her stature was erect, and a little taller than the average height of females. Her countenance and voice were feminine; but she conversed with such ease on the subject of theology, on political subjects, and military tactics, that her manner would seem to be masculine.

We might note the misfortune for women of that day that a lawyer and a senator automatically would consider a woman of intelligence and superior knowledge to be "masculine" in manner.

Ellis concluded nonetheless: "I recollect that it once occurred to my mind that her manner of conversation on any subject embraced that kind of demonstrative, illustrative style which we admire in the able diplomatist."

Diplomat she was. Who else but the most diplomatic of women could have been successful in the venture Deborah Sampson conceived and embarked upon? Diplomat par excellence, with qualities of fortitude, determination, bravery and a blitheness of spirit.

Several years ago the authors started gathering material for this book and visited two of Deborah's great-great-granddaughters in Sharon, Florence Gannett Moody and her sister, Eleanor Moody Connors. Their great-grandfather was Earl Bradford Gannett and they were the cousins of one of Deborah's biographers, Pauline Moody. They graciously displayed Deborah's large wooden cupboard once used as her pie closet and her hutch table that turned into a high-backed chair when the round top was lifted and placed against the wall.

The Historical and Antique Collection at the Sharon Public Library contains a tin foot-stove, nine inches by six inches, donated by Deborah's son, Earl. The shape of a heart is punched in the tin in small holes, which would allow heat to escape from the charcoal burning inside. This collection also possesses a wooden pie crimper made by Deborah and a canteen she used in the war. She gave the canteen to her sister, Hannah Sampson, of Achushnet. It was kept for years by Hannah's grandson, Benjamin Bosworth Hayward. He died May 19, 1902, at the age of ninety-four and his grandson, Benjamin F. Hayward, then gave it to the collection.

There have been a number of memorials to Deborah Sampson Gannett. A World War II liberty ship, the *Deborah Gannett*, slid down the ways of the Bethlehem-Fairfield Shipyard in Baltimore on April 10, 1944. A chapter of the Daughters of the American Revolution is named after her and there is a stone in her honor in the altar of the nation at Cathedral of the Pines in Rindge, New Hampshire.

A bas relief of Deborah with a brief inscription of her military service below adorns a bronze plaque in Rock Ridge Cemetery, Sharon, where she is buried. It was donated by her grandson, George Washington Gay. Other memorials in her name in Sharon include a street, a park and a sparkling spring at the Fish and Game Club, whose property includes the spot on which the Gannett house once stood. During the bicentennial celebration, silk-screen T-shirts bearing her likeness were sold locally.

In Rock Ridge Cemetery under the shade of "the third maple down" lies the grave of Deborah Sampson, between the graves of her husband and her son. One side of her gravestone is inscribed:

DEBORAH
WIFE OF
BENJAMIN GANNETT
DIED
APRIL 29, 1827
AGED 68 YEARS

The other side of the gravestone holds another inscription:

DEBORAH SAMPSON GANNETT
ROBERT SHURTLEFF
THE FEMALE SOLDIER

SERVICE (1781—1783)

There is a special marker beside her grave. The marker designates those who fought in the revolutionary war. She is the only woman in the world to have a revolutionary war grave marker.

A bronze plaque in her honor is imbedded in a boulder set in the middle of the village green at Plympton. It reads:

**IN HONOR OF
DEBORAH SAMPSON
WHO FOR LOVE OF COUNTRY SERVED
TWO YEARS AS A SOLDIER WITH**

WAR OF THE REVOLUTION

**SHE WAS BORN IN PLYMPTON, MASSACHUSETTS
DECEMBER 17, 1760
THIS MEMORIAL ERECTED BY THE
DEBORAH SAMPSON CHAPTER
DAUGHTERS OF THE AMERICAN REVOLUTION
OF BROCKTON AND THE TOWN OF PLYMPTON
1906**

It is reported Deborah's mother always remained ashamed of Deborah. Not only because she joined the Continental Army dressed like a man but because she was expelled from the Third Baptist Church in Middleborough. This is borne out in a letter by Mrs. Zilpah Tolman written in 1902 to Eugene Tappan, first secretary of the Sharon Historical Society.

Mrs. Tolman was the granddaughter of revolutionary veteran Jeremiah Thomas, whose third wife, Sylvia Sampson, was Deborah's niece. Mrs. Tolman reported Sylvia related to her "incidents of the Army life of her aunt and my grandfather as she heard them from her lips." Mrs. Tolman further asserted that Deborah's mother and some of her relatives were "not at all proud of her escapade, but did respect her for keeping her secret intact

and retaining her virtue amid the rough associations which surrounded her."

Sylvia Sampson's version of Deborah's mother is in stark contrast
to the image of the woman who protested, "That's not fair!" when
her daughter said she had been afraid to tell her she had joined the
Continental Army. But if Sylvia Sampson spoke the truth, then
Deborah's mother was to be pitied. She did not realize she had
borne a child who would live forever in the annals of American
history because of her courage. This was the loss of Deborah's
mother, for accepting the hypocrisy of her time.

Deborah apparently agreed with Sylvia's account, for she asked
Mann not to publish his rewritten manuscript about her before her
death, feeling her mother still censured her for what she had done.

In his preface to *Deborah Sampson's Diary of 1802*, which he
borrowed from one of her relatives to make a facsimile by hand so
the Sharon Library would have a record of it, Eugene Tappan
mentions the name of Rhoda Gannett Monk, a granddaughter of
Deborah's.

Mrs. Monk recalled her schoolmates would taunt Rhoda by
calling out, "Your grandmother was a soldier! Your grandmother
was a soldier!"

Indeed she was. America's first official woman soldier. America's first heroine. America's first feminist. Even if her mother
never understood what she had done to become both heroine and
feminist.

But Deborah was a heroine for more than joining the army
disguised as a man. It took someone of her heroic state of mind to
help her country oust the cruel, greedy British, Tories and Indians
who murdered the innocent—those seeking the right to govern
the colonies they had created.

Some of Deborah's ancestors had braved the first visit to America
on the *Mayflower*. Deborah did not wish to see their hard work of

building a new continent destroyed by enemies who possessed the intent to murder. She volunteered to fight as the nation's first feminist, to prove women had the courage to wage war on behalf of their country by the side of men.

She put her early emotional suffering to use in a way that helped save the colonies. Classmates scoffed at her grandchildren, "Your grandmother was a soldier!" But because this grandmother had become a soldier and fought in battles that helped win the war, the dreams of the early settlers in Plymouth and Plympton, as well as the rest of the nation, were able to come true.

Through her courage Deborah Sampson did indeed contribute to the creation of "the land of the free and the home of the brave."

APPENDIX

DEBORAH SAMPSON'S
SPEAKING TOUR AND EXHIBIT
CONDENSED FROM HER DIARY

Deborah Sampson started her speaking tour twenty years after she had first walked into West Point in the guise of a man. She was married and had given birth to three children. The tour was set up for her by Herman Mann, printer and writer. She opened with a performance at the Federal Theater in Boston that ran on March 20, 24 and 27, in 1802. She listed the following dates and places, along with some personal notes:

MAY 3, 1802. Took stage from DEDHAM, MASS TO PROVIDENCE, R.I.

MAY 5, 1802. Exhibited at AMIDON'S HALL IN PROVIDENCE, R.I.

MAY 8, 1802. Took stage from PROVIDENCE to BOSTON, MASS.

MAY 13, 1802. Took stage from BOSTON to SHARON, MASS.

MAY 26, 1802. Rode to DEDHAM, MASS.

MAY 27, 1802. Went to BOSTON with Mrs. Mann. Returned same day, disappointed.

Stayed at home most of month of June.

JULY 3, 1802. Went with her son to Captain James Tisdale in MEDFIELD, MASS.

JULY 7, 1802. Hired horse & chaise and went to SUDBURY, MASS. stayed until Thursday the 8th.

JULY 8, 1802. Took stage to WORCESTER, MASS. Stayed with Mr. Jacob

Biller until Sat morning, July 10th. Hired horse & chaise and went to HOLDEN, MASS. Stayed at Capt. Webb's until July 29th, 1802.

JULY 21, 1802. Exhibited at WORCESTER Court House, MASS.

JULY 30, 1802. Exhibited at HOLDEN, MASS.

AUGUST 3, 1802. Left Capt. Webb. Went to WORCESTER, MASS. Took stage.

AUGUST 4, 1802. Went as far as Capt. Draper in BROOKFIELD, MASS.

AUGUST 5, 1802. Started for SPRINGFIELD, but did not go because of sickness. Went to Mr. William Howe in BROOKFIELD. Stayed until Aug. 9.

AUGUST 10, 1802. Left BROOKFIELD. Went on in the Mail as far as SPRINGFIELD, MASS. to Mr. E. Williams, formerly of ROXBURY, MASS.

AUGUST 13, 1802. Delivered an oration in the Court House, SPRING-FIELD, MASS.

AUGUST 16, 1802. Went from SPRINGFIELD to NORTH HAMILTON, MASS.

AUGUST 17, 1802. Took up boarding in Mr. Pomroy's family until next Sat.

AUGUST 18, 1802. Delivered an oration at NORTHHAMPTON, MASS.

AUGUST 20, 1802. Went to CHESTERFIELD.

AUGUST 21, 1802. Went to PITSFIELD, MASS.

AUGUST 22, 1802. Went to ALBANY, N.Y.

AUGUST 24, 1802. Took up boarding at Mrs. Keeler's in Green St., AL-BANY.

SEPT. 1, 1802. Delivered an address at ALBANY, N.Y.

SEPT. 6, 1802. Left ALBANY. Took stage for SCHENECTEDY, N.Y.

SEPT. 7, 1802. Delivered an address in the Masonic Hall in SCHENEC-TEDY, N.Y., occupied by Mr. James Rogers, where I have taken up board-ing for a short time. This city is located on the west branch of the Mohawk River.

SEPT. 9, 1802. Delivered an oration at BALLSTOWN at the SPRINGS. BALLSTOWN is 8 miles from SARATOGA, 25 from SCHENECTEDY, nearly N.W. from ALBANY, N.Y., 40 miles from Albany, N.Y. Crossed to Mohawk River 20 miles above the forks which are north from ALBANY. After crossing the Mohawk we went through a dismal looking country from ALBANY to BALLSTOWN.

OCT. 10, 1802. Arrived at ALBANY, stayed with Capt. Keeler.

OCT. 11, 1802. Taken very sick. Oct. 12, no better, same Oct. 13, 14, 17.

OCT. 18, 1802. At HUDSON CITY, unwell.

OCT. 20, 1802. Came to CATSKILL.

OCT. 24, 1802. Set out on journey for SKENANGO in Mr. Baldwin's wagon. Arrived at SISWEHANNAH Oct. 30, 1802.

NOV. 1, 1802. Crossed the River at WATEL'S FERRY [now Whiting's Point].

NOV. 11, 1802. Arrived at Judge Patterson's [sic] at LISLE, N.Y.

DEC. 11, 1802. Set out on my journey from LISLE with Judge Patterson [sic] and Mr. Stanley, back to the SISQUEHANNAH. Arrived at WATLE'S FERRY.

DEC. 27, 1802. Still here. Arrived the 14th, put up at Bush's at WATLE'S FERRY.

DEC. 27, 1802. Still at the SISQUEHANNAH. Can't get away because of the weather.

JAN. 2, 1803: No opportunity to go on to New York.

JAN. 2, 3, 4, 5, 1803: Unwell. Sent for Dr. Huntington, fever.

Deborah then listed the "PLACES ETC. WHERE I STAYED SINCE LEAVING HOME," including:

Mr. Robert Williams, BOSTON, MASS. Liberty Square

Mrs. Jones, widow, at PROVIDENCE, R.I.

Capt. John Seamons at NEWPORT FERRY, WARF LANE.

Mr. Herman Mann's at DEDHAM, MASS.

Capt. James Tisdale at MEDFIELD, MASS.

At SUDBURY, MASS. one night [probably Old Howe Tavern, or Red Horse Tavern, now Wayside Inn].

At WORCESTER, MASS. at Mr. Jacob Miller's.

At HOLDEN, MASS. at Capt. George Webb's.

At BROOKFIELD, Mr. William Howe.

At Capt. Draper's at SPRINGFIELD, MASS.

Mr. Eleazear Williams, son of Dr. Williams, formerly of ROXBURY, MASS.

At NORTHHAMPTON, Mr. Pomeroy.

At Mr. Alfred Pomroy at CHESTERFIELD.

At PITSFIELD, MASS. Mr. Allen.

At ALBANY, Capt. Keeler's in Green Street.

At SCHANACTEDY, Mr. James Rogers.

At BALLSTOWN, Mr. MacMaster.

Capt. Ashley at CITY TROY.

Mr. Booth at CITY HUDSON.

Mr. Street in CATSKILL. Left on Friday.

Mr. Bostock, EASTON, MASS.

Mr. Bromhall. REOPCHEG (?).

At NORTH HAMPTON. At Mr. Pomroy's.

At CHESTERFIELD. Mr. Whitemore, then on to ALBANY, N.Y.

At the POOL at BETHLEHEM, where some people were cleansed.

FEB. 23, 1802. At Mr. Graves the 24th.

MARCH 22, 1802. 150 people in the theater, BOSTON FEDERAL STREET THEATER.

JUNE. Arrived at NEWPORT, R.I., very sea-sick. Took stage to BOSTON, MASS. Then took stage to SHARON, MASS.

Deborah also listed the places where she "exhibited":

BOSTON, MASS. at FEDERAL STREET THEATER, March 20, 24, 27, 1802.

PROVIDENCE, R.I. at AMIDON'S HALL, May 5, 1802.

WORCESTER, MASS. at the COURT HOUSE, July 21, 1802.

HOLDEN, MASS. July 30, 1802.

BROOKFIELD, MASS. Aug. 9, 1802.

SPRINGFIELD, MASS. Aug. 13, 1802.

NORTHAMTON, MASS. Aug. 18, 1802.

ALBANY, N.Y. Sept. 1, 1802.

SCHENECTEDY, N.Y. Sept. 9, 1802.

BALLSTON or BALLSTOWN SPRINGS, New York, Sept. 9, 1802.

Her misspelling of the names of some towns has not been corrected. Sometimes she would spell a town's name one way, as with Watel's Ferry, followed by a second spelling, Watle's Ferry. "Siswehannah" was obviously Susquehanna, the 444-mile river flowing through New York, Pennsylvania and into Chesapeake Bay. "Schanactedy" was Schenectady, a city in central New York.

She gave up on "REOPCHEG," listing it with a question mark. Perhaps it was an Indian village, now nonexistent.

BIBLIOGRAPHY

BOOKS

Beard, Charles A., and Mary R. Beard. *The Rise of American Civilization*. New York: Macmillan Company, 1933.

Boynton, Edward C. *General Orders of George Washington Issued at Newburgh on the Hudson 1782–1783*. Harrison, New York: Harbor Hill Books, 1973.

Boynton, Edward C. *History of West Point*. New York: Van Nostrand, 1863.

Cheney, Cora. *The Incredible Deborah*. New York: Charles Scribner's Sons, 1967.

Clapp, Patricia. *I'm Deborah Sampson*. New York: Lothrop, Lee & Shepard Co., 1977.

Dorson, Richard M. *American Rebels*. New York: Pantheon Books, 1953.

Evans, Elizabeth. *Weathering the Storm*. New York: Charles Scribner's Sons, 1975.

Fast, Howard. *Citizen Tom Paine*. New York: Duell, Sloan and Pearce, 1949.

Forbes, Esther. *Paul Revere and the World He Lived In*. New York: Houghton-Mifflin, 1942.

Hale, Sara Josepha. *Woman's Record*. Harper & Brothers, 1855.

James, Edward T. *Notable American Women (1607–1950)*. Cambridge, Mass.: The Belknap Press of Harvard University Press, 1971.

Mann, Herman. *The Female Review or Memoirs of an American Young Lady*. Dedham, 1797.

Moody, Pauline. *Massachusetts' Deborah Sampson*. Privately Published, 1975.

Palmer, Dave Richard. *The River and the Rock*. New York: Greenwood Publishing Corporation, 1969.

Riling, Joseph R. *Baron Von Steuben & His Regulations*. Philadelphia: Ray Riling Arms Book Co., 1966.

Scheer, George F., and Hugh F. Rankin. *Rebels and Redcoats*. New York: The World Publishing Company, 1957.

Thacher, James, M. D. *A Military Journal*. Boston: Richardson and Lord, 1823.

Vinton, John Adams, Rev. *The Female Review, Life of Deborah Sampson, the Female Soldier in the War of the Revolution*. Boston: J. K. Wiggins and William Parson Lunt, 1864.

Wells, Peter. *The American War of Independence*. New York: Minerva Press, 1968.

Wright, Richardson. *Forgotten Ladies*. Philadelphia: Lippincott, 1928.

ARTICLES

Huguenin, Charles A. "Heroine in Buff and Blue." *Westchester Historian*. Vol. 41, No. 2. (Spring, 1965).

Tappan, Eugene. Introduction to the reprint of "An Address, Delivered with Applause." Dedham. 1802. *Sharon Historical Society Publications*, No. 2 (1905).

ORIGINAL SOURCES

Commonwealth of Massachusetts. Documents concerning Deborah Sampson's back pay in 1792, consisting of her petition, a statement by Colonel Henry Jackson, and the muster certificate of Captain Eliphalet Thorp, and the bounty certificate signed by Noah Taft.

First Baptist Church of Middleborough records (Entry September 3, 1782).

Gannett, Deborah. *An Address, Delivered with Applause*, 1802.

Gannett, Deborah Sampson. *The Diary of Deborah Sampson Gannett in 1802*, Sharon Public Library, Sharon, Mass. Hand-copied facsimile.

National Archives. Service file and pension papers of Robert Shirtliff/Deborah Sampson, Rev. Soldier 32722.

Plympton Vital Records, Book 2, p. 718.

Sampson and Thomas family records.

INDEX

ABOUT THE
AUTHORS

Lucy Freeman, author of sixty-nine books, started as a news reporter with the *New York Times*, where she established the mental health beat. She is best known for *Fight Against Fears*, the story of her psychoanalysis, which has sold more than a million copies and is still in print after thirty-nine years. Two of her books have been television features. *Betrayal*, the story of a young woman who sued a New York psychiatrist for using sex as therapy, was shown in 1982 on NBC. *Psychologist with Gun*, written with Dr. Harvey Schlossberg, was the basis of the 1984 television series *Jessie* on ABC.

Ms. Freeman has also written books on true crime, including *Before I Kill More*, the story of a young Chicago murderer, believed the first "whydunit." She is past president of the Mystery Writers of America. Her latest book, *Our Wish to Kill: The Murder in All Our Hearts*, written with Dr. Herbert S. Strean, appeared in April 1991. Among her biographies are *The Story of Anna O*, the woman Freud said led him to psychoanalytic theories, and *Heart's Work:*

Civil War Heroine and Champion of the Mentally Ill, Dorothea Dix, both published by Paragon House.

Dr. Alma Bond, a leading psychoanalyst, is author of *Who Killed Virginia Woolf?*, a psychobiography published by Human Sciences Press in 1990. She is also the senior author of *Dream Portrait*, coauthored by Dr. Daisy Franco and Dr. Arlene Richard. New in psychoanalytic literature, the book deals with nineteen sequential dreams of one patient that led to the successful termination of her analysis with Dr. Bond.

She has also written many professional articles, including "The Masochist Is the Leader," that have appeared in the *Journal of the American Academy of Psychoanalysis*.

Dr. Bond is among the first nonmedical psychoanalysts in the United States to be admitted recently to the International Psychoanalytic Association. She is a Fellow, former faculty member, and training analyst at the Institute for Psychoanalytic Training and Research in New York. She recently moved to Key West, Florida, where she is devoting herself full time to the writing of a novel, *The Quantum Twins*, in which a woman psychologist is one of the two leading characters.

DEBORAH SAMPSON'S ANCESTORS

after Robert Sherman's chart

PLYMPTON RECORDS*
B.2 PP. 540-576-718

BRADFORD BIBLE**
AT PILGRIM HALL

PLYMOUTH RECORDS†

Abraham (brother of Henry) to Duxbury c. 1630

Sampson Highway surveyor 1648
–1690 Constable 1653–freeman 1654

Lt. Samuel Nash 1602–1682

Isaac* Sampson –1726

Esther Nash 1638–1733

Capt. Miles* Standish

Alexander* Standish

Barbara Thorne

John†

Alden

William† Mullins

Alice

Lydia* Standish

Jonathan, sr.* Sampson 1690–1758

Thomas Lucas –1676

Benona Lucas 1659–1730

Sgt. Wm. Harlow

Mary Faunce

Sara† Alden 1629–

Priscilla† Mullins

John Faunce

Patience Morton

Joanna Lucas 1691–1768

Repentance Harlow 1660–1738

m. 1721 Plympton

Jonathan, jr.* Sampson 1729–

Gov. William** Bradford 1588–
m.(2) 1623
Alice (Carpenter)** Southworth

Joseph** Bradford

Elisha* Bradford 1669–1747

Deborah Bradford 1732

m.(2) 1719 Plymouth

Edmund, b. 1574, Hingham, Engl.
Hobart

Margaret m. 1600 Dewey c. 1580–1633

Rev. Peter Hobart*

Rebecca Ibrook –1645

Jael** Hobart

Rev. Peter Hobart 1st minister of Hingham

Elizabeth Ibrook –1645

Israel Hobart 1642–

Sarah Hobart 1670–1704/5

Francis† LeBrock Paris, France

Bathsheba† LeBrock 1703–

Rev. Wm. Wetherill

Sarah Wetherill

m. 1751

Deborah* Sampson 1760–1827